editoria

For the tenth year of *Warship* a few changes have been made. The most obvious will have been noticed already. After five years of colour covers we have commissioned Ross Watton, well known for his 'Anatomy of the Ship' volume on the *Belfast*, to produce four covers specifically for *Warship*. The other major change will not be so attractive. After holding the cover price for the last five years the economics of publishing have forced an increase. Taking a positive view this long delayed rise will ensure that the high standards of the journal are maintained for some time to come.

This issue features three warships that have been preserved. The Chilean *Huascar* and the British *Warrior* were both ships of great significance during their active careers. *Huascar* brought local seapower within the grasp of the smaller nations, in much the same way at the missile-armed fast attack craft of today. The importance of *Warrior* requires no emphasis; as the first and most elegant of the iron battleships she marked the greatest single advance in the evolution of the fighting ship.

By contrast Motor Minesweeper 191 was an auxiliary vessel, with a ̄ ̄ ̄ ̄ ̄ous role. Her preservation will help to emphasise the vital part that she and hundreds like her played in the Second World War.

Another rescue project currently under consideration concerns the Australian Coast Defence Turret Ship *Cerberus*, which was sunk to form a breakwater off Melbourne in 1936. The ship, aptly named after the guardian of the underworld, would certainly make a fitting memorial in the 75th anniversary year of the Royal Australian Navy. It must be hoped that the project will attract the financial and professional support that will be required if it is to succeed.

Cerberus's technical significance lies in her small displacement, powerful armament (4 10-inch muzzle-loading rifles) and her lack of sailing rig. Historically she symbolises a civilian and colonial conception of Imperial strategy that relied on individual isolated units, rather than the main fleet. While she must have provided the citizens of Melbourne with some peace of mind *Cerberus* would have been of little value if the 'enemy' ever gained command of the seas around Australia. Quite who she was built against remains a mystery. The only logical explanation is that the foolish French and Russian naval scares of the period were transferred from Britain, where they were incredible enough, to Australia, where they were farcical. An understanding of strategy was, and remains, vital when warships are ordered.

Andrew Lambert

Cerberus with Lord Brassey's yacht *Sunbeam* in Port Phillip Bay.
CPL

The Ironclad Turret Ship Huascar

by Gerald L Wood,
in collaboration with
Philip Somervell and
John Maber

The Laird-built Confederate Turret ship taken into the Royal
Navy as HMS *Wivern*.

CPL

One hundred and twenty years ago, the small ironclad
Huascar left Birkenhead flying the colours of the
Republic of Peru, bound for South American waters to
counter the threat of a Spanish squadron intent on re-
conquering one of its old colonial possessions. Today,
this relic of another era lies proudly preserved as a
national monument at its moorings at the naval base of
Talcahuano, Chile, 240 miles south of the country's
main port Valparaiso. The *Huascar* means as much to
Chileans as the *Victory* to Britons or the *Mikasa* to the
Japanese. During its 36 years in active service (14 in the
Peruvian and 22 in the Chilean fleets), *Huascar*'s actions
in combat proved an excellent illustration of the
capabilities and limitations of this type of vessel. Its
principal features of armoured protection, firepower
and ramming ability were each demonstrated in the
three major naval encounters of its career.

Named after an Inca chief, son and successor to the

	Huascar	*Bellona**	*Minerva**
Yard no	321	326	327
Purchaser	Peru	Paraguay	Paraguay
Date	1865	1865	1865
Displacement	2030t (max)		
Dimensions lwl/w	184ft/35ft	174ft 4in/35ft	195ft 3in/35ft
Draught	15ft	15ft	15ft
Engine power	300hp	140hp	300hp
Speed	12.277kts	10.5kts	11kts
Turret	1	1	2
Armament	2-300pdr (10in)	2-150pdr (7in)	4-140pdr (7in)
Protection	4.5in	4.5in	4.5in
Turret armour	5.5in	4.5in	4.5in
Ihp	1640	1200	1200
Floated out	7 Oct 1865	Oct 1865	Dec 1865
Completed	Dec 1865	1866	1866
Fate	extant, museum		

*purchased by Brazil in 1865, renamed *Bahia* and *Lima Barros*

11th Inca emperor Huayna Capac, *Huascar* was one of a series of Laird ironclads incorporating the innovative Coles' revolving turret, built for South American squadrons in the 1860s. [see table]

COLES AND THE TURRET

Experience during the Russian war led Coles to criticise the conventional broadside arrangement of a ship's armament, since this made necessary wide ports to permit training of the guns, leaving the guns' crews vulnerable to enemy fire. He proposed instead the mounting of a small number of heavy guns in armoured 'cupolas' or turrets carried on turntables which could be trained on either beam. The turret gun port need be no longer than that required to accommodate the gun while allowing the necessary freedom to elevate. The turrets were to be carried on the upper deck where obstructions were to be kept to a minimum thus to permit the maximum arc of fire. As in the case of Ericsson's 'monitor' concept, a low freeboard was intended to minimise the target presented to an enemy while at the same time reducing the hull weight when compared with that required for a 'between deck' broadside arrangement.

The first warship built to accord with Coles' ideas was launched as *Rolf Krake* for the Danish government by Robert Napier & Sons of Glasgow on 1 December 1862. Of 1320 tons displacement she had a freeboard of only 3ft and carried four 68 pounder smooth-bore muzzle-loading guns in a pair of turrets. Intended for coastal defence, the *Rolf Krake* was provided only with a light three-masted schooner rig.

Similar low freeboard coast defence ironclads were built for Britain and Prussia, but in the meantime Coles turned his attention to the design of a sea-going turret ship. A full sailing rig was required but in order to reduce the need for a mass of standing rigging, which would restrict the arcs of fire of the turrets, Coles designed the lower masts as tubular iron tripods. The first vessels of

Huascar at sea after her last reconstruction, albeit under tow.
Courtesy of Admiral Wood

this type were laid down by Laird Bros at Birkenhead as *North Carolina* and *Mississippi* for the Confederate States Navy in April 1862 but to cover their true identity, arrangements were made fo their 'purchase' on behalf of the Egyptian government! In the event, their intended role could not be concealed so in 1864 they were seized and on completion were taken into RN service, respectively as *Scorpion* and *Wivern*. Both mounted the same armament comprising four 9-inch muzzle-loading rifled (MLR) guns carried in a pair of turrets, forward and aft, at a height of six feet above the water although, as was also the case in the *Rolf Krake*, their sea-keeping qualities were improved by the provision of hinged iron bulwarks, five feet in height, abreast the turrets. When clearing for action these dropped outwards to clear the arcs of fire. Both were barque rigged but tripod fore and main lower masts featured only in the *Wivern*.

HUASCAR

Next in the series of Coles' inspired ironclads came the smaller *Huascar* for which the order was placed on behalf of the Peruvian government in 1864. Of 1101 tons builder's measurement she displaced 2030 tons max in deep condition, and was 200ft in length (bp) by 35ft beam with a draught of 15ft forward and 15ft aft. The hull was protected over the length of the magazine and machinery spaces by a 2in deck and by 4.5in of wrought iron side armour extending to 3ft below the waterline amidships with, forward and aft, a narrowing belt tapering to 2in at the extremities. Fourteen inches of teak backed the side armour. No protection was provided, however, in the way of the funnel uptakes, nor was there any armoured grating to protect the downtakes around the funnel casing. Internal subdivision, apart from the collision bulkhead forward, comprised four transverse watertight bulkheads, the forward one of 4½in iron to protect the magazine and the others, plus longitudinal bulkheads abreast the boiler room, of ⅝in iron plate. A double bottom extended the length of the magazine and machinery spaces.

The first of a series of photographs covering the removal of *Huascar*'s turret. Here one of the 8-inch guns is being lifted through the turret roof.
Admiral Wood

MACHINERY AND TURRET

The propulsion machinery was a Maudsley return connecting rod engine, a modification of the horizontal engine from the old steeple form, by which the same object is obtained as in the Penn trunk engine, viz, a sufficiently long stroke and connecting rod in the narrow cramped space of the hold. By this design the cylinders may be got up close to the turning range of the crank pin and connecting rod heads, and so a longer stroke is obtainable than by any other plan of horizontal engine arrangement. It also had the advantage, besides its compactness, that it could be positioned below the water-line, rendering more protection, reducing top-heaviness, and allowing the propeller to be fully submerged. Other ships of the Chilean navy carried this engine in this period, such as the corvettes *Chacabuco, O'Higgins* and *Abtao*. The first engines of HMS *Monarch* and *Raleigh* were of this type also.

No auxiliary engine was carried initially, apart from a donkey engine for feeding the boilers and pumping bilges. Other pumps were connected directly to the main engine. *Huascar*'s engine was of 1200ihp, built with two independent cylinders 54in by 36in connected to the one crankshaft driving a 170in four bladed propeller at 78rpm. The steam exhausted from these cylinders discharged into two jet condensers. Vacuum was produced by condensation and an air pump placed below the main condensers moved by a piston rod, connected directly to the pistons of the main engines. Four rectangular ('box') boilers generated steam at 30psi; two had four furnaces and the other two had three. Coal capacity of 300 tons permitted, in optimum conditions, cruising for 7½ days at full speed, for ten days at 10 knots, for 12 days at 9 knots, and fifteen days at 5 knots. Under steam, given reasonable weather, the *Huascar* could maintain 12 knots. In addition, she carried sail being rigged as a brig with an iron tripod fore lower mast of Coles' design. Iron wire rigging supported the tubular iron mainmast.

The turret which measures approximately 22ft in diameter, turned on roller bearings, resting on races on the middle deck, and guided by a fixed pivot resting on a bearing riveted to the keel. The turret was rotated manually, taking 16 men 15 minutes to complete the full circle. Owing to the raised forecastle and conning tower and mainmast astern of the turret, its arc of fire amounted to 138 degrees, ie, from 10 degrees either side of the bow line to 32 degrees on either side of the stern line. The turret housed two Armstrong 12 ton, 10in 300-pdr shunted rifled muzzle-loading guns, made in 1865 and numbered 1351 and 1358, mounted on Scott's turret carriages.

The turret was protected by 5½in thick armour, backed by 13in of teak and an ½in iron inner skin. On the turret face, an extra 2in of armour plate was added, and the backing proportionately reduced. The turret roof was of 2in plates. Access to the turret was gained from below and through the roof. A pair of 40-pdr Armstrong guns on the quarterdeck and a 12-pdr at the stern completed the weapon fit.

Abaft the turret, a hexagonal conning tower plated with 3in armour backed by 8 inches of teak stood 7ft 6in high from the deck. On top sat the bridge. Forward a 6ft high top-gallant forecastle carried the anchor gear and from this structure aft to the mainmast there were hinged iron bulwarks, dropped down when clearing for action. From the mainmast aft the bulwarks were of wood and fixed. The bow itself was shaped and strengthened for ramming.

ACQUISITION

Amidst a flurry of intensified European interventions in the Western hemisphere, with France attempting to install a monarchy in Mexico, and Spain 're-annexing'

The second gun being lifted clear.
Admiral Wood

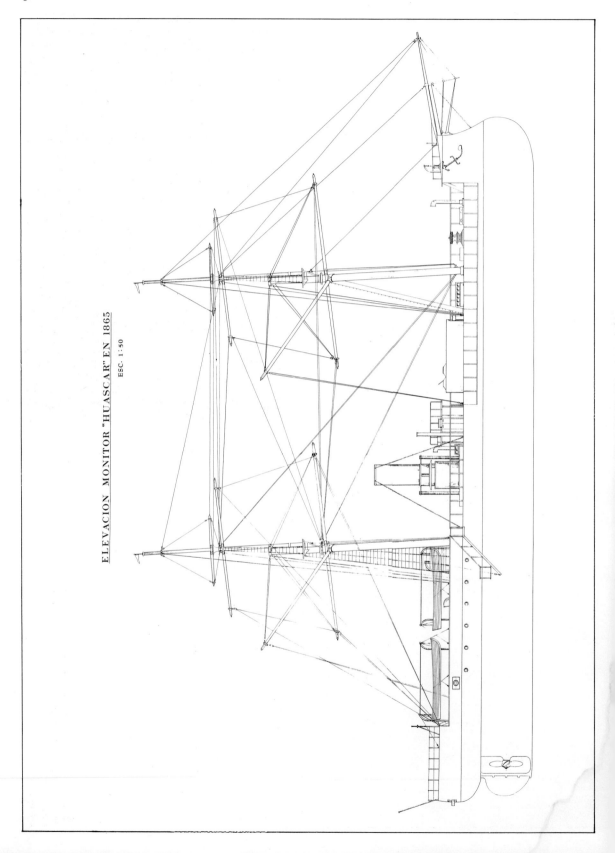

ELEVACION MONITOR "HUASCAR" EN 1865

ESC. 1:50

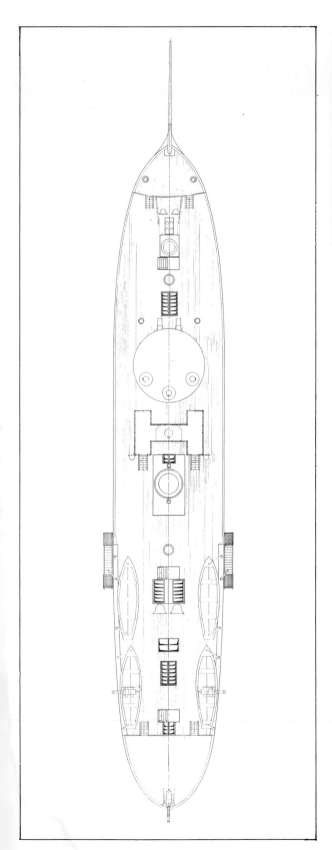

*Huascar as completed in 1865.
Drawn by Vice Admiral Wood*

The empty turret. Hinged iron bulwarks originally ran from the forecastle to the superstructure aft of the turret to preserve seaworthiness.
Admiral Wood

2

3

1 Lifting the turret.
Admiral Wood

2 The turret ashore. The curious angle is caused by the central
support, visible over the stern of the 'O'Higgins' class cruiser.
Admiral Wood

3 The ship without her turret. Note the roller path on the lower
deck.
Admiral Wood

1

1 The roller path, the central support ran through the centre of the deck to the keel.
Admiral Wood

2 *Huascar* under reconstruction in dry dock at Talcahuano. The underwater plating has been removed to reveal the frames.
Admiral Wood

3 A stern view, showing the method of stowing the boats and the port side sponson for the secondary armament.
Admiral Wood

3

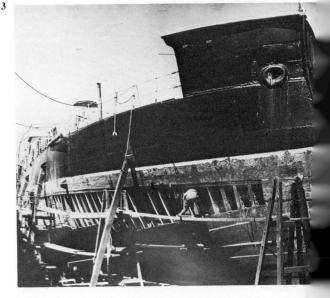

Santo Domingo, in addition to uneasy relations between the three Pacific coast states of South America, Peru, Bolivia and Chile concerning ill-defined boundaries in the northern Atacama region, a Spanish squadron comprising eight warships (207 cannon) under Admiral Alvarez, seized the guano-rich Chincha islands in southern Peru in April 1864. Alvarez demanded payment of 3 million pesos outstanding debts. Alvarez' successor Admiral Pareja, in 1865 turned his attentions to Chile, announced a punitive blockade of Chilean ports and in March 1866 turned his cannon on the commercial port of Valparaiso, inflicting considerable damage. A subsequent quadruple alliance deprived him of a Pacific port of shelter; after skirmish actions against the allied squadron, the South American commanders took the defensive, in expectation of the arrival of warships from

2

Europe. After failing to penetrate the defences of Callao (Peru), Pareja quit the coast in May 1866.

The naval squadrons of Peru and Chile in the early 1860s scarcely merited the name. Chile's 18-gun wooden screw corvette *Esmeralda* and a four-gun steamer were matched by Peru's steamers *Amazonas* and *Apurimac*, wooden screw frigates. Experiences of the American Civil War highlighted the apparent value of the monitor and small commerce raiders as inexpensive alternatives to ships of the line. Chile in the first instance opted to purchase four 'Alabama-type' steamers to be built at Laird's, while Peru chose to acquire two different vessels, sending separate naval commissions to Europe in 1864. In the event, Chile desisted, preferring two wooden screw corvettes (*O'Higgins* and *Chacabuco*, R H Green at Blackwall, 1864-67). Peru ordered a Coles single turret ship from Lairds', the *Huascar*, and a broadside ironclad frigate, *Independencia* from Samuda on the Thames. In addition, Peru secured two Confederate corvettes, embargoed during the Civil War by the French, *Texas* and *Georgia* (renamed *America* and *Unión*). Chile was subsequently offered an improved version of *Huascar* in 1868 by Laird, a twin screw, twin turret (Coles), incorporating better protection and higher freeboard on a larger hull, for £112,000, but refrained from the purchase, owing to economies, and only later ordered two central battery ironclads, in 1872.

DELIVERY

Huascar departed Birkenhead on 17 January 1866, under the command of Captain José María Salcedo, a Chilean officer in the service of Peru, in great trepidation at the prospect of being seized by the British authorities who would enforce a neutrality provision in the impending state of war between Spain and Peru. *Huascar* entered Brest harbour on 23 January to await her companion *Independencia* and supplies of coal and munitions. After overcoming delays in port, the two ships collided at sea, with substantial damages to bulwarks being sustained, which had to be repaired at Funchal (Madeira). A collier, *Thames*, joined the convoy at Cabo Verde. *Huascar* suffered further damages with the loss of a propeller blade, in mid-Atlantic. This did not impair her performance unduly, for Salcedo succeeded in taking two prizes of Spanish brigs laden with cargo, scuttling them both after calling at Rio de Janeiro. A third Spanish vessel was seized by *Independencia* and joined the convoy through the Straits of Magellan, where their new escort, *America* was met. At Ancud, southern Chile, *Huascar* joined the Chile-Peruvian allied squadron (Chilean Rear-Admiral Manuel Blanco Encalada's flag flying on *Unión*), whereupon Salcedo was appointed to command the Peruvian division. After calling at Valparaiso on 15 June, *Huascar* steamed north to Callao, where hostilities with Spain had already terminated.

to be continued

The Old 'S' class destroyers 1939-45

by Mark Brady

Shikari ca 1930 as control ship for the radio-controlled target ship *Centurion*
Wright & Logan

INTRODUCTION

This article is in effect a sequel to that by Commander Malleson in *Warship* 16, for I believe that he did not say enough about the service of the 'S' class destroyers in World War II. He wrote of the class as a whole, of course, and by 1939 most had been scrapped. Those which did survive (along with *Skate*, the sole survivor of the 'R' class, which for all practical purposes was grouped with her 'S' class half-sisters after the outbreak of war) had fairly undistinguished wartime careers. None the less, a study of the service of these old destroyers between 1939-45 is not only interesting in itself, but also leads one to a more general conclusion – that it is not sufficient for a navy to possess warships; there must also be a clear idea of their intended purpose. From the end of the First World War the Royal Navy had little use for its existing 'small' destroyers, and rightly concentrated upon development of the 'fleet' type – the 'V & W' class and their successors of the 'A' to 'I' classes. (The later 'Hunt' class – in which speed and torpedo armament were sacrificed to achieve good gunpower on a 'small' hull – represented a departure from 'traditional' thinking in that respect, although their design can also be seen as a *revival* of the 'small destroyer' concept.)

Other navies continued to make good use of 'torpedo boats' displacing about 1000 tons in their well-established 'offensive' role: the Royal Navy's use of the 'S' class in 'defensive' roles during World War II had little effect, as will become apparent.

DESIGN

In many respects the design of the 'R' and 'S' class destroyers pre-dated the First World War. The Admiralty 'R' class, of which *Skate* was one, were essentially repeats of the Admiralty 'M' class (of the 1913–14 Programme), the only significant difference being that the Admiralty 'R' class had geared-turbine main machinery. As a result of war experience it was thought that sea-keeping qualities would be improved if the forecastle were extended aft. Eleven Admiralty Modified 'R' class were therefore built with the boiler rooms transposed, allowing the designers to combine the uptakes from two boilers, move the bridge and 'A' gun aft, and lengthen the forecastle. The Admiralty 'S' class were repeats of the Admiralty Modified 'R' class, the most obvious difference (after removal of the single 18in TT under the bridge) being the increased sheer of the 'S' class forecastle and its 'semi-turtleback' form.

It is important to stress that these were boats designed for war in the North Sea. Their weight was initially limited by the stipulation that the floating dock at Harwich was to be able to lift two 'M' class, and the weight limitation effectively limited their dimensions. Later the urgent need for destroyers dictated that design changes should be kept to the essential minimum: the 'M', 'R' and 'S' classes were mass produced with the clear understanding that to have a large number of adequate destroyers was more important than building larger boats of improved design, because the latter course would mean that fewer boats could be built. As it was, the 'M' class and their derivatives were fast, handy and were well-armed by the standards of the time. Their seaworthiness and endurance were considered adequate for operations in the North Sea; but by the end of 1916 it was recognised that a larger destroyer was preferable for work with the Grand Fleet, which the C-in-C had decided to keep at a grater distance from U-boat bases. For that reason the 'V' and 'W' classes, designed originally as 'leaders', were built as fleet destroyers. Construction of the 'R' class (and their 'S' class successors) continued because they could be built quickly and in large numbers.

Before considering their service in World War II, therefore, it is essential to recognise that those 'R' and 'S' class destroyers which survived in 1939 had been retained far longer than had been envisaged when they were built. Indeed, they had been retained far longer than was prudent in an era when improvement in warship capabilities almost invariably entailed increase in weight. The fact that after 20-years life their hull and

Sabre in November 1937. Demilitarised as a target ship. Aircraft torpedoes (with inert heads) were dropped against the ship itself; practice bombs were aimed at a towed target.
Wright & Logan

machinery were in good condition is of less importance than the tacit acknowledgement prior to the outbreak of war that few changes could be made to these small destroyers to fit them for front-line service. (Some 'V & W' boats, on the other hand, were extensively modified before the war as AA escorts. Others were retained as destroyers, and were later modified as ASW escorts.) Those 'R' and 'S' which did survive to serve in the 1939-45 war were, therefore, 'thrown to the wolves' to a certain extent.

As had been the case when they were built, they are available, even if not ideal for their intended role; but by 1939 time had passed and the nature of maritime war had changed.

PRE-WAR PLANS

Before the outbreak of the Second World War the Admiralty had no plans to use the 'R' and 'S' class destroyers in the event of war with Germany and/or Italy except in subsidiary roles, despite the expectation that the Royal Navy would be greatly stretched. There were plans, however, to form a flotilla of 'S' class destroyers in the Far East.

Simultaneous war with Germany, Italy and Japan was the nightmare of British strategists in the late '30s: it was recognised that British forces could never be adequate for that eventuality. As prolonged war with Germany became increasingly likely, therefore, Britain's posture in the Far East changed. British strength would be reduced from a level adequate to hold out until reinforcements arrived to that sufficient to defend British

1 *Sardonyx* in April 1938, as a tender to the Signal School. There is a DF
loop aft (above the after pair of TT), with the control cabin immediately
abaft.
Wright & Logan

2 *Scimitar* in April 1939. The derrick on the forecastle is possibly for the
recovery of practice torpedoes.
Wright & Logan

interests in 'peacetime'.

Part of that scheme was the replacement of a flotilla of relatively modern destroyers on the China Station (the 'D' class) by eight 'S' class boats, which would form the Singapore and Hong Kong Local Defence Flotilla. Normally armed as destroyers, all these boats were to be capable of laying mines at short notice (as certain of the class had been in the 1914-18 War). In that event they would land the after 4-in gun and the after set of TT to compensate for the added weight of 40 mines. They were also to be fitted with ASDIC, but otherwise were only to be overhauled to restore them to running condition. They would, therefore, be sent out much as they had been when first built.

It was intended that *Scout, Thanet, Thracian, Tenedos, Stronghold, Sturdy, Saladin* and *Sardonyx* would be sent to the Far East. Left at home would be *Shikari* (control ship for the Fleet Target *Centurion*), *Sabre* (de-militarised as a Torpedo Bomber Target) and *Scimitar* (based at Portsmouth 'for RAF Reconnaissance duties' – probably an aircrew training role). In addition there was *Skate*, the sole surviving 'R' class boat, serving as a tender to HMS *Vernon*, the Torpedo School. For some years *Skate* had been fitted for minelaying training and trials, for which reason she had outlived the rest of her class.

As it happened, five of the intended eight destroyers went to the Far East. Of the others, all except *Sturdy* (lost in 1940) were converted as ASW escorts and served with Western Approaches Command. It is therefore logical to discuss the boats (excepting *Sturdy*) in two main groups.

FAR EAST DESTROYERS

By September 1939 *Scout, Thanet, Thracian* and *Tenedos* had joined the Eastern Fleet, and were serving in Chinese waters. Later that year *Stronghold* was sent out; she arrived at the end of 1939 and was based at Singapore. *Sturdy* was delayed because on being taken out of Reserve she was found to require extensive re-wiring; *Saladin* was also delayed, for boiler re-tubing in her case. *Sardonyx* was to be refitted for service in the Far East on completion of Signal School trials of the prototype 50cm gunnery radar[1], but before completion of her refit France had fallen and Britain's situation was so serious that no destroyer, however obsolescent, could be spared from home waters.

The strength of the Hong Kong and Singapore Local Defence Flotilla therefore remained at five 'S' class. No significant improvements were made to those boats before the Japanese struck in December 1941. *Thracian* was wrecked at Hong Kong during the defence of the colony, and was later salved by the Japanese and used as an escort. *Scout* and *Thanet* left Hong Kong before its surrender, to join *Tenedos* and *Stronghold* at Singapore. *Stronghold* and *Thanet* were sunk in separate actions with Japanese warships in the first months of 1942; *Tenedos* was sunk by carrier aircraft during the Japanese attack on Colombo. Of the five ships, therefore, only *Scout* survived the Japanese onslaught. From April 1942 until the end of 1943 she served as an escort for traffic between Aden, Bombay and Ceylon, being based at Colombo. She was fitted with Type 291 radar in 1943, but otherwise was not significantly modified. From December 1943-February 1944 she was refitted at Colombo, and was thereafter used as an Air Target Ship. In the spring of 1945 she was decommissioned, and placed in Care and Maintenance Reserve at Trincomalee[2].

HMS STURDY

Sturdy was taken out of Reserve in the summer of 1939 to be refitted for service in the Far East but the work took longer than was anticipated, as mentioned above. Toward the end of 1939 she was dispatched to the Far East through the Mediterranean, but while en route was ordered to join the Mediterranean Fleet as a 'planeguard' to the aircraft carriers. (This was a duty which a number of 'R' and 'S' class boats had performed between the wars: their speed and handiness made them very suitable for recovery of ditched aircraft and aircrew.) After the defeat of France and the outbreak of war with Italy, however, *Sturdy* was recalled home to join the 22nd DF at Portsmouth (see below). Like the other boats of the 'S' class in home waters she carried out anti-invasion patrols and was then lent to Western Approaches Command. She took part in one convoy battle (the defence of HX 79) before being wrecked on Tiree at the end of October 1940. She was armed similarly to the boats in the Far East; between her return from the Mediterranean and her unfortunate loss there was no opportunity to make any modifications.

ASW ESCORTS

As stated above, there were no plans in 1939 to use those 'R' and 'S' class boats which would be retained in home waters for anything other than subsidiary roles. After the end of 1939, however, no more old destroyers were sent to the Far East. Remaining in home waters were *Shikari* and *Sabre* (effectively without armament); *Skate* (permanently fitted for minelaying); *Saldin* (her refit for service in the Far East extended for boiler retubing) and *Sardonyx* (refitting for the Far East after completion of Signal School radar trials); and *Scimitar*. Only the last named carried full destroyer armament.

During the winter 1939-40 *Skate* and *Scimitar* were employed in minesweeping trials, as tenders to HMS *Vernon*[3]. *Shikari* (after re-arming) and *Saladin* (on completion of refit) joined the 16th DF, the Portsmouth Command local flotilla. *Sabre* continued as a target until she ran aground on the Scottish coast early in 1940. She was salved, and sent to Grangemouth for repairs and refitting. *Sardonyx*'s refit had comparatively low priority. During the 'phoney way' period, indeed, there was no urgent need to refit any of these old ships for war service. The Royal Navy was having sufficient difficulty in manning and equipping new ships, and in repairing weather or battle damage to operational vessels.

March's *British Destroyers* refers to *Skate* being fitted with enhanced AA armament (one quadruple, 2-pdr and two quadruple in 0.5in MG) in 1940, and to a proposal to refit *Sabre* for magnetic minesweeping and as an AA escort[4]. I believe that the intention was that

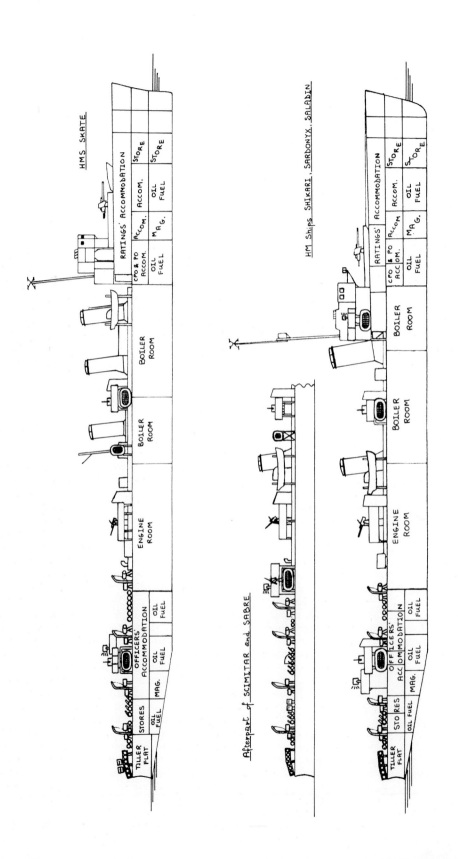

The ASW conversions.
Drawn by the Author

Skate in July 1936, with mines embarked.
Wright & Logan

they should escort coastal convoys. (Moreover, as will become apparent, I believe that employment as coastal escorts would have been the best use of those 'R' and 'S' class remaining in home waters.) However, I have not seen a photograph of *Skate* with the armament mentioned. As she was converted as an ASW escort in the summer of 1940 I rather doubt that she ever carried a quadruple 2-pdr.

March does not explain why *Skate* and five of the 'S' class (*Scimitar, Shikari, Sabre, Saladin* and *Sardonyx*) were converted as ASW escorts in the second half of 1940, despite his remark that 'they worked far out into the Atlantic escorting convoys, loaded down so heavily that their rolling was terrible.' I do not subscribe to the theory that the Admiralty was irredeemably stupid. Nor, I think, did March. But a weakness of his immense and fascinating work is that he often quotes information uncritically, without evaluating it or specifying his source. His implicit assumption that his sources were comprehensive and irreproachable cannot, sad to say, be accepted once one realises how many errors and omissions he made.

That said, the need for ASW escorts was, of course, pressing as the prospect of another U-boat campaign against shipping in the North Atlantic became a reality. I cannot believe, however, that the Naval Staff would seriously have considered using those small destroyers in the Western Approaches. My own view is that the proposal to remove most of their existing armament and to install what was, on the face of it, very formidable anti-submarine armament was taken at a lower level. The

first two ships to be converted were *Skate* and *Scimitar*[5], both tenders to the Torpedo School, and in my opinion the conversion was typical of those often proposed by naval officers without consulting naval architects – too much armament was added with too little regard for stability and seaworthiness! Two single 4-in guns and their ammunition, both sets of torpedo tubes[6] and some superstructure were removed; but far more weight was added. With two DC rails and eight throwers a 14-charge pattern could be fired, and the outfit of charges allowed eight of such patterns – 112 depth charges. The DC alone weighed some 25 tons, without considering the weight of the rails, throwers and handling gear. In addition, one 12-pdr AA and two quadruple 0.5in MG were added, and ASDIC was fitted to those boats not already equipped. The addition of weapons and other equipment required increase of complement, of course – by 1943 some 130 men were living in spaces designed for 89, with severe overcrowding on the ratings' messdecks.

The slender hulls of these small destroyers, already overloaded during the ASW conversion and soon to be subjected to the full rigours of service in the North Atlantic, allowed little in the way of further wartime improvements. Type 286 radar was added in 1941[7], but the S-band Type 271 could not be fitted – the additional topweight was unacceptable, as was the risk of damage to the aerial from the heavy seas that frequently swept over the bridge. Only *Shikari* was equipped with S-band radar – Type 272 was fitted aft in 1944 (after removal of the 3in AA gun and reduction of the ASW armament). Lack of centimetric radar, of course, seriously reduced their value as convoy escorts.

Some improvements, however, were felt to be essential. The quadruple 0.5in MG mountings were removed,

1 *Scimitar* as a unit of 21st EG 1942-43. Compare with p260-1 of *Warship* 16, showing the same ship on completion of ASW conversion.

Author's Collection

2 *Sabre* in November 1944, fitted for mine countermeasures trials. Armament considerably reduced (compare with *Scimitar*), after funnel remains cut down.

MoD

and replaced by four single 20mm. VHF tactical radiotelephone, additional lifesaving gear and extra protection for upper-deck personnel were also added. Furthermore, it was possible to reduce the weight of armament without loss of effect. Trials in 1942 established that a modified 10-charge DC pattern was actually more effective than the 14-charge pattern (*Skate* was one of the ships engaged in those trials). Four throwers and their handling gear could therefore be removed, and the DC outfit reduced, without reducing the number of attacks that the destroyers could make. Later in the war, once they were employed closer to the British Isles (ie in shallower water) it was no longer necessary to fire 10-charge patterns – a 5-charge pattern was adequate, allowing further saving of weight. The 3in AA gun, which had always been carried as a deterrent rather than in the serious hope of hitting aircraft, was also removed from some of the boats later in the war.

Another improvement worthy of note was the replacement of Mk II DC throwers (which required an expendable carrier to be attached to each charge) by the Mk IV model (with integral carrier). As consequence a 'parbuckling' stowage/loading system replaced the tall handling davits, making reloading of the throwers much safer in a seaway.

However, one must bear in mind that the improvements that allowed weight to be reduced came only slowly. By 1943 the full-load displacement of these ships had risen to nearly 1400 tons. As built it had been 1220 tons, and that was 100 tons more than the designed full-load displacement of the 'M' class. On assuming command early in 1943 the CO of *Shikari* found that in seagoing condition she floated 18in deeper than designed, and that almost all the extra weight had been added at upper deck level or above[8]. Perhaps the substitution of heavy ASW armament in place of guns and torpedoes had been considered acceptable in view of the fact that the 'R' and 'S' classes had been used as minelayers. It is true that the maximum mine load (40 mines) weighed about the same as 112 DC. Minelaying, however, required no increase in complement – and the deadly cargo was usually only given a one-way trip! *Shikari*'s CO requested an inclining experiment when his ship was refloated in dock (and therefore, presumably, in light condition without fuel and armament). Her GM was found to be 4in. That, of course, was not the GM in seagoing condition. But, when short of fuel but carrying a full load of DC, one would not expect these ships to be fit for service in the North Atlantic.

Nonetheless, after *Skate* and *Scimitar* had been converted similar alterations were made to the other four ships by the end of 1940. All six initially joined the 22nd DF (Portsmouth Command), loaned to Western Approaches Command for escort duties in the North Atlantic. On account of their short endurance (Lenton quotes 2750/1215 miles at 15/24 knots, but probably less as displacement increased) they were usually based in Londonderry, sometimes in Iceland.

Throughout 1941 they were allocated to various escort groups; but in company with larger or more seaworthy escorts they suffered a lot of weather damage from being driven too hard, or just from the normal hazards of life in the North Atlantic. One reads of regular damage to bridgework and loss of ships' boats, and there must have been doubt as to whether these boats were being properly employed. At the end of 1941 it was decided that the six ships should be brought together to form the 21st EG; as a homogenous group under a Senior Officer aware of their problems it was hoped that the old destroyers would give better service. Even so, they continued to spend an excessive amount of time under repair – which made them popular with their crew[9] but did not get the war won! One should not be surprised that all six survived the war, despite their being engaged in the Battle of the Atlantic from mid-1940 to the autumn of 1943. Until the end of 1941 they figure occasionally in accounts of the battle, but once formed into the 21st EG they received little further mention[10]. (It is only fair to state, however, that after the entry of the USA into the war the U-boats concentrated first off the east coast of North America and later in the mid-Atlantic 'Gap', out of range of shore-based aircraft. From the end of 1941, therefore, the action moved beyond the range of the old destroyers.)

In the waters between the British Isles and Iceland the 21st EG may have had fewer chances to fight U-boats during 1942-43 but the weather was a constant enemy. After Operation *Rosegarden* failed in the summer of 1943[11] because the old destroyers were unable to cope in the prevailing weather it was acknowledged that before the next winter they had to be found less arduous employment. In the autumn of 1943 the 21st EG provided attack and evasion training for submarines, escorting 'enemy' convoys in the Clyde Exercise Areas, but at the end of 1943 the group was dispersed.

Sardonyx and *Shikari* remained in the Clyde area until the end of the war in Europe, attached to the 3rd Submarine Flotilla as local escorts and to provide training. *Sabre* became a tender to HMS *Vernon* and carried out minesweeping trials (probably acoustic and pressure-mine sweeping and countermeasures trials) in the Firth of Forth and off the east coast of Scotland. She also remained in commission in May 1945. *Saladin*, *Scimitar* and *Skate* were attached to Plymouth Command at the end of 1943 as local escorts. Throughout 1944 they were employed in the preparations for the Normandy invasion, during the landings themselves and latterly as escorts for cross-Channel movements. In December of that year they de-stored at Milford Haven and were subsequently put into Category 'C' Reserve at Falmouth.

CONCLUSIONS

The war service of the 12 ships was not impressive, notwithstanding some battle honours and the loss of five of their number. That should not be surprising, of course, for they had been retained to fight in a war very different from that for which they were designed. But was it inevitable that they should be of indifferent value?

Those ships sent to the Far East could not reasonably

Saladin in March 1943. *Sardonyx* and *Shikari* were of similar appearance.
MoD

have been expected to have survived in the event of war with Japan. The Admiralty was aware of that, but to send them out was none the less a reasonable decision. Reduction of the fighting strength of the Eastern Fleet not only allowed modern ships to be concentrated in European waters but was also a conscious signal to the Japanese that Britain was most anxious to avoid war.

Those which remained in home waters, however, could have better employed. They were fast and handy ships, in good condition, but their armament was weak and their endurance limited. They were seaworthy enough for the North Sea, but too small for the North Atlantic. They were also too small to allow any overall increase in weight without sacrificing speed or seaworthiness. It follows, therefore, that the decision to convert them as ASW escorts was unwise. It was inevitable that such a conversion would entail increased weight, and that once converted they would subsequently be employed in the Western Approaches, where the battle against the U-boats would have to be fought. Why were they not used as escorts for East Coast convoys instead?

The explanation that in the second half of 1940 there was such a crying need for ASW escorts that any destroyer was better than none is a poor one. Firstly, there was no convincing reason for using 'R' and 'S' class boats in the Western Approaches and the larger 'V & W' class in the North Sea – any rational man would take the opposite decision. Secondly, on a more general note, it is a recurring lesson from military history that equipment which is inadequate for its task is actually worse than none at all (because there is then a tendency to undertake operations which have a high risk of failure, whereas even the most unwise commander will not make plans dependant upon units which do not exist). The

decision to convert them as ASW escorts must have been taken without much consideration. Indeed, the original suggestion probably came from outside the Admiralty and was subsequently 'nodded through' during a period (spring and summer of 1940) of confusion.

To state that the six ships converted as ASW escorts were mis-employed for much of the war is not merely wisdom after the event. The principles determining the seaworthiness and stability of warships were well known in 1940, or should have been. Modernisation requires careful thought. It is not just a question of removing old equipment and installing new: one must also think about the intended role of the modernised ship and ask oneself whether she will be able to perform that role adequately. Too obvious? I can think of recent cases in which that simple principle has been ignored.

I do not accept Cdr Malleson's concluding implication that modification of these small destroyers for service in World War II was a waste of resources. I would not go so far as to suggest that more should have been retained – indeed, it would have been wiser to let more of the 'S' class go to scrap and retain more of the 'V & W' class. Nor would I claim that the ASW conversion was a success – patently it was not. However, given that *Skate* and a number of the 'S' class were available at the start of World War II, I think that they ought to have been put to better use. I would venture to suggest that they might have been put to better use had officers of the Royal Navy made more careful study of naval history and naval architecture!

Shikari in 1944-5. Note single DC rail and two throwers (five-charge pattern); throwers are Mk IV, with adjacent 'parbuckling' stowages for DC. Note also removal of 3in AA gun, after pair of 20mm moved forward.
Author's Collection

BATTLE HONOURS

Sardonyx

Atlantic	1940-32
Arctic	1942

Sabre

Dunkirk	1940
Atlantic	1940-43

Scimitar

Dunkirk	1940
Atlantic	1940-44
Arctic	1942
English Channel	1943–44

Saladin

Dunkirk	1940
Atlantic	1940-44
Arctic	1942-43
English Channel	1944

Shikari

Dunkirk	1940
Atlantic	1940-43

Skate

Atlantic	1940-44
Arctic	1943
English Channel	1944

Notes:

1. See p 175 of *The Electron and Sea Power* by Vice-Admiral Sir Arthur Hezlet. The 50cm radar pioneered by the Signal School was developed as Types 282-5.
2. March states (*British Destroyers* p223) that *Scout* served in the North Atlantic. The 'Pink Lists', however, show that she remained in the Far East.
3. See p 32-3 of *Allied Minesweeping in World War 2* by P Elliott. A number of magnetic sweeps were tried, but one conclusion was that magnetic minesweeping could not be done at speed. It followed that destroyers were not really suitable for the task.
4. See p 186 of *British Destroyers*. The reference to *Sabre* arises from a mis-reading or mis-spelling, I am quite sure. *Sable* was scrapped in 1937, whereas *Sabre* was indeed docked at Grangemouth early in 1940.
5. *Skate* was taken in hand in May(?) 1940 and was ready for service early in August. *Scimitar* was converted as she underwent repair after the Dunkirk evacuation, completing early in September 1940. The remainder were, I believe, converted before the end of 1940.
6. In *Scimitar* and *Sabre* a deckhouse replaced the after set of TT (the photo on p 262 of *Warship* 16 is of *Sardonyx*, not *Sabre*). *Skate* and the other three 'S' class had a deckhouse built over the after steering position. It may have been intended that some or all of those four should be able to re-embark torpedo tubes, provided that the two forward paris of throwers and their handling gear were removed: In 1940–41 the threat from surface raiders was still real. The 'Pink Lists' refer to retention of TT by *Shikari* as late as January 1943. The original intention, however, was that all six ships should be able to drop a 14-charge DC pattern; and I believe that they were all equipped to do so during

their conversions. I have found no firm evidence that any of the ASW conversions retained TT, or ever re-embarked them.
7. There is a poor photograph facing p 32 of *Convoy Escort Commander* showing *Sabre* with a fixed forward-facing aerial for Type 286 at the foremast-head; but most photographs show these ships with the latter (and lighter!) X-shaped Type 286P/Type 291 aerial.
8. Rayner p 131-2.
9. Rayner p 132-3. Admiral Gretton paints a somewhat less gloomy picture of *Sabre* in 1941, but there can still be no doubt that these ships were too small for the North Atlantic. Perhaps *Shikari* was unlucky – if these accounts are to be believed she lost her after funnel on at least two separate occasions!
10. I consulted Roskill's *War at Sea* and Rohwer & Hummelchen's *Chronology*. Incidentally, I found no reference to any Arctic service, despite four of the ships having that Battle Honour.
11. Rayner p 140-150. *Rosegarden* was the German nickname for the British deep minefield between Iceland and the Faeroes. The plan called for the 21st EG and other destroyers to patrol the minefield in conjunction with Coastal Command aircraft, forcing U-boats in transit either to dive and risk the mines or to stay on the surface and be attacked. Unlike similar joint ASW operations in the Bay of Biscay at that time, Operation *Rosegarden* was a failure.

Sources

The War at Sea Capt S Roskill
Chronology of the War at Sea J Rohwer & G Hummelchen
British Destroyers E March
Ships of the Royal Navy J J Coledge
British Fleet and Escort Destroyers H T Lenton
Escort Cdr D Rayner (CO of *Shikari* and SO 21st EG January-October 1943)
Convoy Escort Commander Vice-Adm Sir Peter Gretton (CI of *Sabre* January 1942–January 1943)
The Royal Navy and the Sino-Japanese Incident 1937—41 M Brice
The War Against Japan (Vol 1) Maj Gen S W Kirby
Admiralty 'Pink Lists' and 'Particulars of Warships'
'British A/S Weapon Development 1939-45' A Hague (Article in WSS *Warship Supplement* No 69)

1 *Skate* in 1942. Note tall DC-handling davits, tube stowages adjacent to throwers, DC on quarterdeck with 'stalks' attached.
Author's Collection

2 *Sardonyx* in November 1944. Although a rather murky photograph one can see that the two forward pairs of DC throwers have been removed, and the after pair of 20mm have been moved to the space vacated. The 3in AA gun has also been removed, and torpedo davits (for the recovery of submarines' practice torpedoes) have been reinstated.
MoD

1

2

The USS Long Beach after her 'mid life conversion'

by Wilhelm Donko

The first nuclear-powered surface ship of the US Navy was laid down on 2 December 1957 . Originally to be named *Brooklyn* this was changed later to *Long Beach*. Twenty years after commissioning the ship underwent a 'Mid Life Conversion' which altered her appearance and prepared her for the next 20 years.

Authorised in FY (Fiscal Year) 1959 the cruiser was launched on 14 July 1959 at the Fall River Shipyard (Bethlehem Steel) in Quincy, Mass, already classified as CGN-9. At first the Navy had problems with the classification: from CLGN-160 on 15 October 1956 to CGN-160 on 6 December 1956 a new number system for guided missile cruisers was started in July 1957 and the USS *Long Beach* became CGN-9 (on 1 July 1957.)

A few weeks before the first nuclear aircraft carrier CVAN-65 *Enterprise*, the new cruiser was commissioned at the Boston Naval Shipyard (NSY) on 9 September 1961 for the 2nd Fleet, homeported at Norfolk, Va; Captain E P Wilkerson in command.

As a single ship with a very striking appearance, the first cruiser constructed after World War II, and the first nuclear powered surface warship, the *Long Beach* has become well known all over the world. This article will not deal with the long and famous history of the ship, but with the circumstances leading up to her two overhauls in the 1980s.

In the early 1970s first plans for conversions of *Long Beach* were made. The Navy wanted to rebuild her as a strike cruiser (CSGN) equipped with the most modern weapons and electronic systems available at that time. For $763 million from FY 1977, 1978 and 1979 a nearly new ship should have been built, outfitted with the new Aegis system (for $265 million), the aborted 8in MCLWG (Major Caliber Lightweight Gun) Mk 71 and cruise missiles.

CGN-9 *Long Beach* at San Diego, Ca in August 1980 after part I of the modernisation.

2

1 The well known bridge of CGN-9 still with SPS-32/33 radar; the bridge structure is seven decks high and equipped with an elevator (San Diego August 1980).

2 The use of light metal allowed the enormous dimensions of the superstructure. These materials have proved to be very dangerous for ships in case of battle damage or accidents. (San Diego, August 1980).

3 The square stern of *Long Beach* with Mk 141 Harpoon missile launchers having replaced Talos. The platforms for the former dimmers are empty. (San Diego, August 1980).

1 The two twin Mk 10 Standard launchers are now the only anti-aircraft missile system on board. Eighty missiles can be stowed in the larger magazine for the forward launcher, 40 for the second launcher. The structure of the large magazine can be seen very clearly. (San Diego, August 1980).

2 Three years later – in July 1983 – again at the North Island Naval Air Station in San Diego, where the ship is based; CGN-9 after part II of the 'Mid Life Conversion' showing her present appearance.

3 The superstructure from port; note the new lattice mast with SPS-49 and the tripod mast over the bridge. (San Diego, July 1983).

4 The 'new' bridge now without SPS-32/33 radar. The four SPG-55A dimmers are converted for use of Standard ER missiles and now terms SPG-55B. (San Diego, July 1983).

All photographs taken by the Author

4

All elements of the midship section survived the conversions, including the two old Mk 30 5-inch guns with their Mk 56 fire control and the Mk 16 ASROC launcher; originally this part of the ship was intended to receive the Regulus missile system. (San Diego, July 1983).

1

2

1 The radar equipment: 3-D-radar SPS-48C and navigation and sea control radar SPS-10/65 on fore--TACAN URN-25 in topmast, and the 2-D-air control radar SPS-49 on the lattice mast. (San Diego, July 1983).

2 The two-deck-high Talos magazine remains a prominent feature of the stern section; note the two 20mm Mk 15 Phalanx CIWS. (San Diego, July 1983).

3 Compare these two photographs, taken August 1980 and July
& 1983 in San Diego. In the first picture the hinges are still on
4 the doors of the Talos magazine, after part II of the conversion they have been welded closed.

5 CGN-9 after conversion. (San Diego, July 1983).

A radical overhaul was necessary as her weapons and electronics did not meet modern demands, as for example the obsolete Talos long-range anti-aircraft defense missile system. But the ship was still considered to be very useful, especially as there was an extreme shortage of nuclear-powered surface ships capable of escorting the increasing number of nuclear aircraft carriers. The $783 million Strike Cruiser Conversion would have been the best solution; the Navy would have got a highly modern Aegis ship with nuclear propulsion for relatively low cost, compared to new construction.

But the entire programme became a victim of naval policy during the Carter administration. Instead of the excellent CSGN plans a scanty conversion – in two parts – was undertaken. Between January and April 1979 part

Stern and quarter of *Long Beach* as modernised. (San Diego, July 1983).

I of this conversion took place at the Puget Sound NSY in Bremerton, Wa. The Talos missile launcher was removed as well as the associated radar and electronics (SPS-49, SPW-2); two quadruple Harpoon launchers Mk 141 were placed in the position of the former Mk 12 twin launchers. The platforms of the former dimmers remained empty, the well known SPS-32/33 radar 'plates' – only used in *Long Beach* and *Enterprise* which caused their unusual bridge structures – remained on board. In this configuration the cruiser went back to the home base San Diego, Ca, took part in two exercises with the Canadian Navy and went to Southeast Asia in January 1980 (for her ninth cruise), where she saved 144 boat people off Vietnam.

From 6 October 1980 to 13 March 1983 part II of the 'Mid Life Conversion' took place, again at the Puget Sound NSY. This second part was much more intensive than part I: a new lattice mast was set up on top of the former Talos missile magazine bearing the air control radar SPS-49; two Mk 15 Phalanx guns were also mounted on top of the magazine.

The bridge got a new tripod mast with the 3-D-radar SPS-48 and navigation radar SPS-10; the SPS-32/33 antennas were removed. Additionally two ECCM systems SLQ-32 (V)-3 and two OE-82 satellite communication antennas were fitted over the bridge as well as TACAN URN-25; the bridge received armour plates. Besides new electronics – specially for the NTDS (Naval Tactical Data System) – the new SQQ-23 sonar was built in. The ship was fitted out for a fleet staff of 10 officers and 58 men, probably in the former Talos magazine. The two old Mk 30 5-inch guns have survived all conversions.

The exact costs for the conversion are hard to determine as it was not paid by regular SCN means for new construction but by a general fund for conversions.

Estimates are between 300 and $350 million (compared to the building cost of $333). The Navy could not expect more than it finally got for this money: the 17,350 ton cruiser does not have much more weapons and electronics than other nuclear-powered ships of half her size (compare CGN-25 *Bainbridge*). The *Long Beach* is ready for the next 20 years but the Navy missed an excellent opportunity to get a nuclear-powered Aegis strike cruiser.

Bridge structure (San Diego, July 1983).

Kitakami

by Hans Lengerer, Sumie Kobler-Edamatsu and Tomoto Rehm-Takahara

Oi, a sister of *Kitakami*, also converted into a torpedo cruiser although seen here in her original configuration.

Author's Collection

THE ORIGIN OF THE 5500 TON CRUISER

As an answer to the very large naval expansion programme of the USN in 1916 (the Navy Appropriation Bill became a law by the act of 29 August 1916) by which the Navy of the USA was authorised to lay down within three years ten BBs, six BCs and 140 ships of other classes, the 8-4 Fleet Completion Programme of the IJN was adopted during the 39th special meeting of the Diet (23 June to 15 July 1917) on 14 July. It allowed the construction of 63 warships (quite contrary to the huge programme of the USN only three BBs and two BCs were included) within seven years. To cover the building costs the Diet authorised expenditure of 265,521,160 Yen.

Of the nine CLs provided under this programme eight finally belonged to the 14 CL's of the so-called 5500 ton class while one unit, known under the name *Yubari*, was

an experimental cruiser. The planning of these ships had begun shortly after the design for the *Tenryu* class, the first modern CLs of the IJN, had been finished. Originally the programme had contained three cruisers with a displacement of 7200 tons and six of the *Tenryu* class (3500 tons) but the planning had been altered at the end of 1917 in favour of ships whose tonnage lay about in the middle between 3500 tons and 7200 tons and that could fulfil the tasks foreseen for the first type (flotilla leader) as well as those of the second one (scouting). Therefore the 5500 tons class was borne.

The fore-mentioned 14 CLs can be divided into three groups:

Group one: *Kuma, Tama, Kitakami, Oi, Kiso.*
Group two: *Nagara, Isuzu, Natori, Yura, Kinu, Abukuma.*
Group three: *Sendai, Naka, Jintsu.*

Excluding the experimental cruiser, the remaining eight units of the 8-4 Fleet Completion Programme formed the five ships of group one and the first three ones of group two.

The building dates of the units of group one are given

in table 1. Their main technical data can be found in table 2. Generally speaking these ships were an improved *Tenryu* type with heavier armament, increased speed and larger radius of action made possible by the larger displacement.

This article will deal only with the conversions of *Kitakami,* undoubtedly one of the most converted ships of the IJN, with a career varying from Light Cruiser to Torpedo Cruiser and finally Kaiten Carrier.

MODIFICATIONS BEFORE HER CONVERSION INTO A TORPEDO CRUISER

Before her conversion into a ship with a heavy torpedo armament (Juraisokan = in the following called Torpedo Cruiser) *Kitakami* had only been slightly modified. The modifications were mostly in the fitting-out but one of structural nature was also carried through. The reason for this had been the capsize of TB *Tomozuru* in March 1934 and the incident involving the Fourth Fleet in September 1935. The reason for the other modifications had been the technical development that was used to improve the fighting strength. Sources do vary regarding the date the alterations took place but have been checked with all available Japanese sources like *Kaigun Zosen Gijutsu Gaiyo, Nihon no gunkan, Showa Zosenshi, vol 1* data in *Sekai no kansen Maru Special, Fune no Kagaki* etc. Despite this, the date (not the data) cannot be considered completely accurate.

When completed her armament included two type 3 machine guns (Kiho). They were replaced by two 7.7mm MG (Kishu) type Ru (or Tome) in about 1928.

The superstructure between the fifth and sixth 14cm gun had been used as mine stowage at the time of completion. When the ships of the *Kuma* class were equipped with a scout plane it was converted in to a hangar for the dismantled seaplane. Before launching the parts had to be taken on the shelter deck by the aircraft derrick, put together and the seaplane brought to water. In the photos of *Kitakami,* taken in 1935, the derrick is not visible indicating that the seaplane was no longer used.

In October 1926 the Minister of the Navy had ordered the investigation of the catapult and in 1928 the compressed-air-driven catapult type Kure no 1 was ready. In the following years other types were developed and became operational. Up to 1935 all ships of the 5500 ton class, except *Kitakami, Oi* and *Kiso,* had been equipped with a catapult.[1]

The funnels were equipped with caps in about 1929/30, quite different to the large caps in *Kuma* and *Kiso*; the other ships, and also of course the *Kitakami,* received caps, whose construction was much more compact.

The aerial of the direction finder, installed between the fifth and sixth 14cm gun, was square at the time of completion but was replaced by a loop aerial in about 1934.

The bulwark that had ended before the aft TT mounts was lengthened to finish behind them in 1934.

The second and third funnels were lowered in 1934/35.[2] Of all cruisers of the 5500 tons class with three funnels, only the *Kitakami* had her funnels lowered.

Therefore she can easily be distinguished from her sisters.

Additional fighting tops and look-out stations were fitted on her main mast. The fire direction equipment was enlarged. The searchlight platforms on her main and fore masts were modified.

New look-out stations were fitted on both sides of the bridge in 1934/35.

The cover of the compass bridge was made from canvas (one source says wood) until 1935/36. At this time it was made from steel and atop it a 4m rangefinder was installed. It replaced the formerly used 2.5m rangefinder.

Her hull was strengthened and measures carried out in order to improve her stability in 1934/36.

The mixed burning boilers were replaced by oil burners in 1937.

The 8cm AA guns were replaced by two twin mounts 25mm MG after 1937.

As a consequence of these modifications the displacement rose to more than 6000 tons, the draught was enlarged and freeboard became smaller. The seaworthiness was adversely affected and the speed reduced to 33.6 knots. But this meant no decisive loss of quality for the 5500 tons class. Drawing no 1 shows *Kitakami* in 1935.

CONVERSION INTO A TORPEDO CRUISER

On 28 November 1935 the IJN officially adopted the oxygen-driven type 93 61cm torpedo. It had been developed in secrecy. With a speed of 48 knots its range was 22,000m, at 40 knots of 32,000m and at 36 knots the range rose to 40,000m. The warhead contained a load of 490kg explosive. This torpedo was the secret weapon of the IJN and one of which they were very proud because it offered the possibility of winning the decisive battle against the main force of the USN. With its range of 40,000m it outranged the main guns of the BBs of the USN, that reached no more than 32,000m.[3]

A glance back on the strategical and tactical planning in the IJN shows that the USN was the hypothetical enemy number one since the end of the Meiji Era (1868-1912). The IJN developed a number of strategies and tactics against the overwhelming strength of the USN and the last conception can be summarised as follows:

The enemy fleet would sail across the Pacific in order to attack the IJN whose task was to defend the Japanese homeland. During the advance the numerical superiority of the USN would be reduced by a number of attacks by submarines and aircraft of the IJN. After that the decisive daylight gunnery action between the main forces of the opposing fleets would take place. In order to improve the possibility of winning the decisive battle the formation of the US Battle Fleet would be thrown into confusion immediately before or during the first minutes of the gunnery action by torpedo attacks. Moreover its strength should be reduced further.

To this end a number of torpedo attacks during the night before and at dawn of the day of the gunnery action were planned. One of the many operations which aimed to reduce the numerical superiority and confuse the US

TABLE 1: BUILDING DATES OF THE FIRST GROUP OF THE 5500 TONS CLASS CLS

Name	Estimates	Lay down	Launched	Completed	Building yard
Kuma	1917	29.8.1918	14.7.1919	31.8.1920	Naval Arsenal Sasebo
Tama	1917	10.8.1918	10.2.1920	29.1.1921	Mitsubishi, Nagasaki
Kitakami	1918	1.9.1919	3.7.1920	15.4.1921	Naval Arsenal Sasebo
Oi	1918	24.11.1919	15.7.1920	3.10.1921	Kawasaki, Kobe
Kiso	1918	10.6.1919	14.2.1920	4.5.1921	Mitsubishi, Nagasaki

TABLE 2: MAIN TECHNICAL DATA OF CL KITAKAMI

Item	Completion	Torpedo Cruiser As completed	As in March	Kaiten Carrier 1944
Displacement				
Standard (tons)	5100	5860		
Normal (tons)	5500			
Trial	5499	6900	7041	7008.6
Main dimensions				
Length above all (m)	162.15			
Length in the waterline (m)	158.53			159.8
Length between perpendicular (m)	152.40			
Beam, max	14.25	17.45		
Moulded depth	8.84			
Draft mean (Trial conditions)	4.80	5.6		
Machinery				
Number and type of machinery	4 Gihon (Gijutsu Honbu) Impulse reaction single geared turbines	4 same type		2 same type
Horsepower (shp)	90,000	77,989		35,110
Number of shafts	4	4		2
Designed speed (kts)	36	–		–
Actual speed (91,108shp)	35.36	31.67		23.81
Boilers (Kanpon type N.B)	10 oil (6 large, 4 small) 2 mixed	12 oil		12 oil
Fuel (tons)	1260 oil 350 coal	?		?
Radius of action (nm/knots)	5000/14	4,000/14		?
Armour				
H(igh) T(ensile) Steel, side (mm)	63.5			
deck (mm)	28.6			
Armament				
LA gun	7 × I 14cm L/50 Model 3	4 × I 14cm	same	nil
HA gun	2 × I 8cm L/40 Model 3	nil	nil	2 × II 12.7cm 40cal
AA MG	2 × 1 three year type later replaced by 2 × 7.7 MG	2 × II 25mm MG	2 × III 25mm MG 2 × II 25mm MG 1 × I 13mm MG	12 × III 25mm MG type 96 31 × I 25mm MG type 2
Radar	nil	nil	nil	1 × No 22, 2 × No 13
Torpedo tubes	4 × twin six year type (53.3cm)	10 × quad type 92 model 3 mounts	8 × same	
Torpedoes	16 × six year type	40 × type 93 modification 2	32 × same	
Mines	48 × type I Gō (No 1)	nil		
Depth charges	nil	18		18
Kaiten	nil	nil		8 × model 4 (planned) or model 2
Aircraft (dismantled)	1	nil		nil
Crew				
Complement	450 (planned)	468 (planned)		615 (planned)

1 Tests were made with Kaiten model 1
2 Some sources do give the number as 27

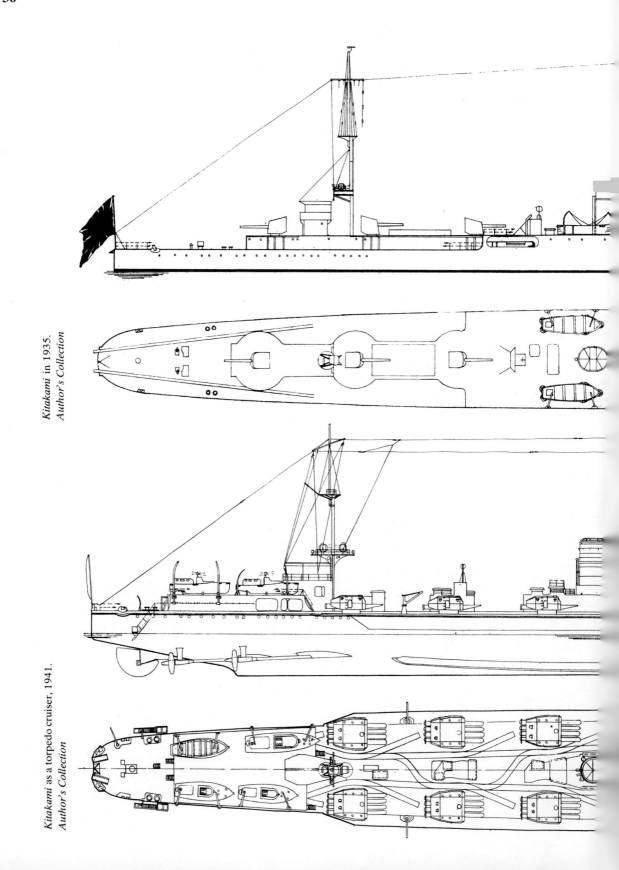

Kitakami in 1935.
Author's Collection

Kitakami as a torpedo cruiser, 1941.
Author's Collection

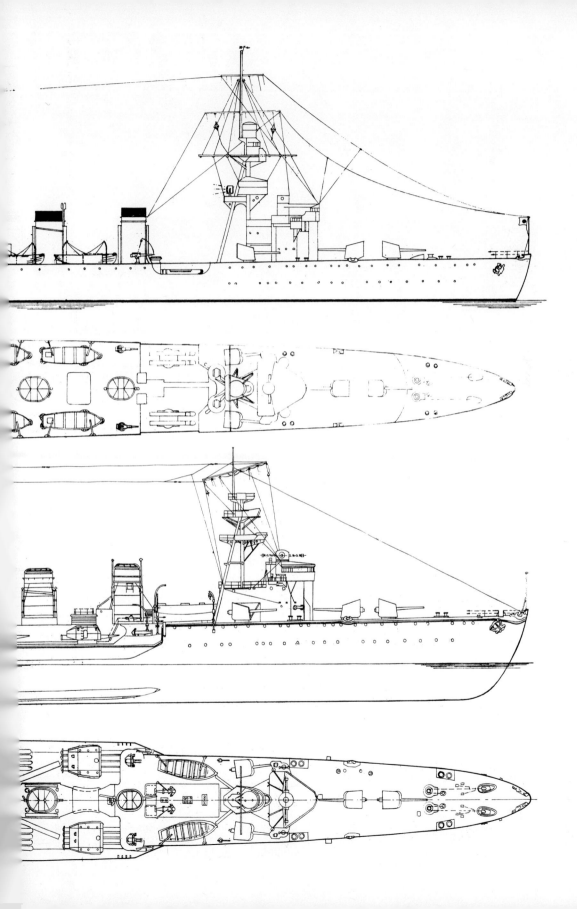

Kiso, another sister of *Kitakami*. She was also scheduled to be converted into a torpedo cruiser, but the conversion was never carried out.

Author's Collection

Battle Line shortly before or immediately after the beginning of the gunnery duel was the so-called 'Torpedo firing operation from great range under great secrecy'. The operation was quite contrary to earlier torpedo tactics. Until the approval of the wakeless type 93 torpedo the torpedo-carrying ships had to approach as close to their target as they could in order to assure a hit. It was now decided to fire a large number of torpedoes out of the range of the old BBs with 35.6cm and 40.6cm guns. When the new BBs with 40.6cm guns appeared the elevation became greater and therefore the range longer. The attack was therefore likely to be a complete surprise and, because of the high speed of the torpedo and the enemy's inability to take evasive manoeuvres, a large number of hits that would reduce further the difference in strength between the opposing forces.

In the course of these deliberations the idea of the ship with a heavy torpedo armament, the 'Torpedo Cruiser', was conceived. Because it would carry as many TT mounts as possible, it was planned to fit such a ship with the quadruple type 92 TT mounts and to equip with 40 type 93 torpedoes (no reserve torpedoes). To realise this idea the 5500 ton class CL was chosen. Because a large fighting power was wanted three ships should be converted.[4] To keep the idea secret in order not to lose the element of surprise it was decided to convert the ships into Torpedo Cruisers only immediately before the outbreak of hostilities.

The conversion programme for three ships (*Kitakami, Oi, Kiso*)[4] was officially included in the Calling-up Preparation Programme (Shusshi Junbi Keikaku) for fiscal year 1937 for the first time[5] and continued in the succeeding programmes. The concept was to start the con-

version immediately when the order for carrying-out the programme had been given. Secret plans were to be drawn up and the material made available in order to speed up the work. In reality the preparation for the conversion did not begin before 1938.

At this time the Sino-Japanese Conflict had widened to an undeclared war, the Russo-Japanese relations had become strained and the USN had begun their Fleet Extension Programme known in Japanese naval circles as the Second Vinson Trammell Plan. In view of the situation around Japan and the Sino-Japanese conflict the IJN started the 'Third War Armament Preparation Programme' (Senbi Sokushin) on 28 October 1938. In this programme it was decided to prepare 22 quadruple TT mounts, eight 12.7cm AA guns and eight 25mm MG double mounts for the cruisers.

While the preparation of the 22 TT mounts was for the Torpedo Cruisers this is only true to a certain degree for the AA guns and MGs.

These were preparations for two ships instead of three. One either supposes that they were to be fitted with 11 quadruple TT mounts, four 12.7cm AA guns and four 25mm Mk in double mounts each, or that two TT mounts were reserve.

On 16 August 1940 a conference between members of the Naval Ministry and the Naval General Staff took place. In the course of it definitive measures were decided in order to speed up and complete the War Armament Preparation Programmes. With regard to the Torpedo Cruisers the following data were given:

Kitakami should be converted into a ship with heavy torpedo armament (possibly replaced by *Kuma*).

Oi was to be repaired according to special rules and converted into a ship with heavy torpedo armament.

Kiso was to be converted into a ship with heavy torpedo armament, but the start of the conversion would be decided later.

On 15 November 1940 the first stage of the Calling-up Preparation Programme (Shusshi Junbi Keikaku) was ordered. At the same time the order for the conversion of *Kitakami* and *Oi* was also given. For their conversion the 76th session of the Diet (December 1940-March 1941) an expenditure of 13,655,000 Yen within the scope of the so-called conversion programme.

The Sasebo Naval Arsenal started the conversion of the *Kitakami* into a Torpedo Cruiser in January 1941. The ship was handed over to the fleet on 25 December 1941. From 20 November it formed, together with *Oi* that had been converted by the Maizuru Naval Arsenal from January to September 1941, the 9th Cruiser Division, serving as flagship.

A number of differences are visible between drawing no 1 and 2, that shows the *Kitakami* as a Torpedo Cruiser.

The main guns were reduced from seven to the four, concentrated in the fore part of the ship.

The four 53.3cm double TT mounts and the two 7.7mm MG were removed.

The crew quarters located on the main deck in the vicinity of the funnels were removed and the beam of the main deck in the middle part (from first funnel to the pole mast aft) enlarged for about 1.6m at each side in order to get a platform for the new main weapon.

Five quadruple type 92 TT mounts along with transport rails for loading the torpedoes into tubes were installed on each side and the centreline respectively. Each tube was located with a type 93 60.9cm torpedo whose speed, range and wakeless track made it to one of the most formidable weapons. Thus the Torpedo Cruiser became something new and unique amongst the warships of the world in carrying such a heavy torpedo armament.

The form and location of the ventilation trunks for engine and boiler rooms, as well as galley, had to be altered as a result of the installation of the torpedo tube mounts.

The superstructure was lengthened behind the pole mast aft. It was used as crew room and the top as a boat deck (one 11m launch, two 9m motorboats, one 8m cutter).

The bridge aft was altered.

The gap between mainmast and first funnel (formerly the position of the first 53.3cm TT mounts) was closed by a superstructure and the bulwark. The room was most probably used as crew space.

The aft part of the bridge was enlarged and used as an operation room.

The location of the fire director, the firing command post and the aiming post for the main guns was altered as were the lookout stations.

The 4m rangefinder was replaced by a 6m.

On a platform of the pole mast two 90cm searchlights were installed while before only one was there.

CONVERSION INTO A TRANSPORT

The forming of the 9th Cruiser Division that belonged to the First Fleet had been a strategical decision. The Torpedo Cruisers were to operate with the Capital Ships and secretly fire their formidable long range wakeless oxygen-driven torpedoes at the best opportunity during the first stage of the decisive daylight gunnery duel. The scenario for the 'Torpedo firing operation from great range under great secrecy' was as follows:

In the night before the decisive daylight gunnery action the US fleet would be subjected to numerous torpedo attacks, from the units of the Advanced Force (Zenshin Butai). This force would be made up of one Kosokusen-kanbutai high speed BB (reconstructed *Kongo* class), one Junyokansentai (CA), one Juraisokansentai (Torpedo Cruiser). Two Suiraisentais (DesRon) would also be a part of the Advanced Butai.

All ships except the high speed BBs were to fire their torpedoes immediately on closing the US main force after the Japanese BBs, whose guns outranged those of their American counterparts, had opened fire.

If the attack order had been given by the Commander-in-Chief, the Fast BB Division was to speed up, destroy and pierce the defence ring protecting the enemy main force, hence allowing the cruisers to get the best firing position. The cruisers should approach obliquely, cross the enemy course and fire the first salvo of torpedoes at a range of 35,000m, ie outside the range of the American guns. While the CAs released the second salvo soon afterwards it was planned to fire the (second) 60 torpedoes of *Kitakami* and *Oi* somewhat later. The fire power of the originally planned three ship Division was equal to those of 15 BB's. The Japanese therefore expected a large increase in attack strength.

As mentioned before, it was expected that the large number of torpedoes (at this stage about 230) would cripple the US main force, sink some BB's and cause confusion in the battle line. But when the conversion of the *Kitakami* and *Oi* had been completed the era of the decisive gunnery duel between battlefleets of the opposing forces was over for ever. The main forces in the sea battle were the aircraft that had taken over the role of the BB. The concept of the decisive gunnery action was now antiquated and without any value. Ironically the strategy of the decisive battle had been out-moded. The IJN that transformed *Kitakami* and *Oi* into Torpedo Cruisers discovered the value of aircraft by the destruction of the US Battle Fleet at Pearl Harbour and the sinking of BB *Prince of Wales* and BC *Repulse* during the first days of the war in the Pacific.

The battle for Midway – the long expected decisive battle – ended with a serious defeat of the IJN which lost four of their best CVs and most of their qualified personnel. After that there was no chance for *Kitakami* and *Oi* to operate according to their conversion roles. They sailed back with Fleet Admiral Yamamoto's Combined Fleet to Hashirajima. After the landing of US forces at Guadalcanal both ships were shifted to Truk where they were used for transport operations in the Southwest Area. At the end of September 1942 two TT mounts were removed[6] (the aft ones) and replaced by some 25m MK in triple mounts. The aft part was used as stowage for some 14m special transport boats (Daihatsu). Afterwards *Kitakami* and *Oi* acted as high speed transports.

At that time the IJN had no high speed transports capable of carrying-out transport operations in areas of enemy air supremacy. Because there had been no opportunity for *Kitakami* and *Oi* to operate as Torpedo Cruisers once the chance for the decisive battle had received until autumn 1942 the most heavily armed Torpedo Cruisers of the world had served as transports. On 19 November 1942 the 9th Cruiser Division was disbanded, and the task of the Torpedo Cruisers ended too.

In 1943 the importance of transport operation grew. In May 1943 the conversion of *Kitakami* and *Oi* to high speed transports was discussed in the Naval Technical Conference and by June a conversion programme had been worked out. It contained the following alterations:

All but two TT mounts were to be removed.

All 14cm guns should be removed and replaced by 12.7cm AA guns.

The turbine sets in the foremer main engine room (two for the outer propellers) and four boilers in the first boiler room should be removed because the ships did not need to be as fast as CL. The rooms were to be used for storage. Furthermore, part of the first boiler room should be used to house a water tank. Because of the removal of the boilers the first funnel was to be dismantled.

The position of the bridge should be altered and a new bridge erected.

The ships were to be equipped with the derricks of AV *Chitose*[7] class which were necessary for taking over the load.

Some Daihatsus (special transport boats) should be carried.

The transport capacity was to be about 300 tons.

This was a large conversion and the number of working days (Kozu) was estimated to be 50,000 (one day = 8.5 working hours), and the time at least five months. In the middle of 1943 there was no building capacity left to do this conversion work. At that time planning and construction of specially designed fast transports had already started and therefore this programme was not realized.

The operation of *Kitakami* and *Oi* as transports continued. On 1 July 1943 they were transferred to the 16th CruDiv belonging to the Southwest Area Fleet based at Singapore. In January 1944 *Kitakami* transported army soldiers from Singapore to Port Blair. On the way back to her base on 27 January she suffered two torpedo hits from the British SS *Templar* and was moderately damaged. Until 21 June 1944 she was temporarily repaired by the 101st Repair Section at Singapore and returned afterwards to Japan.

Kiso in 1932. Note the modified funnels.
Author's Collection

A kaiten being launched from the special sloped stern ramp of *Kitakami*. The officer with two white torpedo stripes around his cap is the famous authority on the IJN Shimazo Fukui.

Author's Collection

THE LAST TRANSFORMATION: CONVERSION INTO A KAITEN CARRIER

On August 1944 the Sasebo Naval Arsenal started to repair *Kitakami*. The IJN took this occasion to convert the Torpedo Cruiser and Transport into a Kaiten Carrier. On 20 January the transformation was finished. Because *Oi* had been sunk by torpedo hits of USS *Flasher* on 19 July 1944 only the *Kitakami* was used for the training of the kaiten crews on sea, to act as target ship for Kaiten attacks and to attack the enemy invasion force with kaiten during the decisive battle for the mainland of Japan (Honshu). Drawing no 3 shows *Kitakami* as a kaiten carrier. The main differences are:

The superstructure in the vicinity of the funnels was widened and mostly used as crews space. Atop it 25mm MGs in triple mounts were installed.

The quarter deck was sloped down to the waterline at the after end for launching the new main weapon. The stern was lengthened at both sides.

The bulleyes were either closed or drastically reduced as a consequence of many war lessons.

The aft part of the platform constructed for the TT mounts was shortened.

The main machinery of the *Kitakami* had been damaged by the torpedo hits of the British SS. During the conversion only the turbines for the outer propellers were repaired and the turbine sets for the inner propellers (aft engine rooms) removed. This was now to be used as stowage room. The output was reduced to 35,100shp and speed to 23 knots. Nothing remained of the high speed that had been a feature of this class.

The 14cm guns and all TT mounts were removed and replaced by two 12.7cm AA gun double mounts and 67mm MG (12 triple mounts and 31 single mounts).

Two depth charge rails with six depth charges each were installed on the stern and atop the superstructure behind the pole mast two depth charge loading frames with three depth charges each and two temporary designed type 3 charge throwers were installed.

It is most probable that this equipment, either partly or completely, was installed during the time the *Kitakami* was used as a high speed transport.

One surface search radar (No 22) was fitted. The aerial was installed atop the main mast. Two air search radars were also installed. Their aerial was mounted at the yard of the main and pole mast.

From the first funnel afterwards to the sloped-down stern two rails were fitted at both sides each of the main deck in order to stow the kaitens. They were transported on special carriages to the stern and launched during full speed of the mother ship. Eight kaitens were distributed evenly on both sides and their launching took no longer than eight minutes. The *Kitakami* was equipped with model 1 kaitens but the stowage room was also constructed for the larger models 2 and 4. But these models never became operational.

The bridge construction was altered and enlarged.

The directing equipment for AA guns was reinforced. The 6m range finder was replaced by a type 94 AA 4.5m rangefinder.

At the pole mast a 20 ton derrick (possibly a 30 ton derrick) from the *Chitose* class was installed.

The number of ship boats was reduced to four (9m life cutter, 9m cutter, 11m motor boat, 11m special transport boat).

In January 1945 the *Kitakami* under the command of the Combined Fleet was shifted to the Japan Sea in order to train kaiten pilots. In April the ship was placed under the command of the 11th DesRon and continued to train the pilots for this suicide weapon. At the end of May they formed with *Natzukaze* and *Namikaze* the Kaijo Teishin Butai that was to carry out surprise kaiten attack against the enemy invasion force. Because of the lack of fuel, training could only be done at anchor. On 1 July 1945 the *Kitakami* shifted to Kurahashijima because of the intensity of the US air attacks. On 24 July 1945 more than 100 carrier-based planes bombed this area and the *Kitakami* was badly damaged by more than ten near misses. Cracks appeared in her hull and the machinery was put out of action.

After the war *Kitakami* was used as repair ship for the special transport ships (formerly warships of the ex IJN) that were used to transport Japanese soldiers and naval personnel from the outward bases back to the Japanese homeland. Stricken from the register of the IJN warships on 20 November 1945 she was towed to the Bay of Kagoshima at the end of 1945 and further used until June 1946 as a repair ship. Afterwards she was towed to Nagasaki where the Mitsubishi Yard started to dismantle her in July 1946. The breakers finished their work on

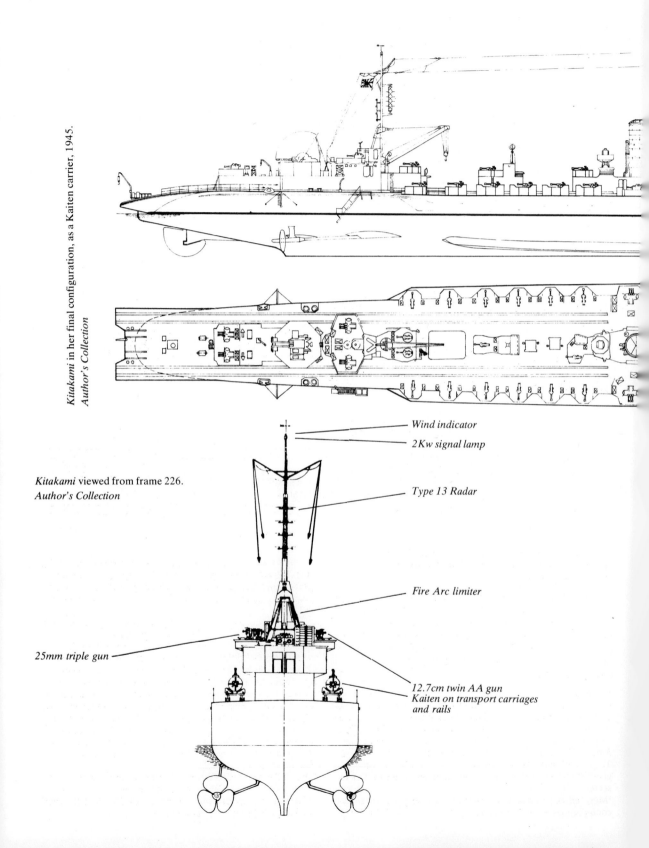

Kitakami in her final configuration, as a Kaiten carrier, 1945.
Author's Collection

Kitakami viewed from frame 226.
Author's Collection

Wind indicator

2Kw signal lamp

Type 13 Radar

Fire Arc limiter

25mm triple gun

12.7cm twin AA gun
Kaiten on transport carriages
and rails

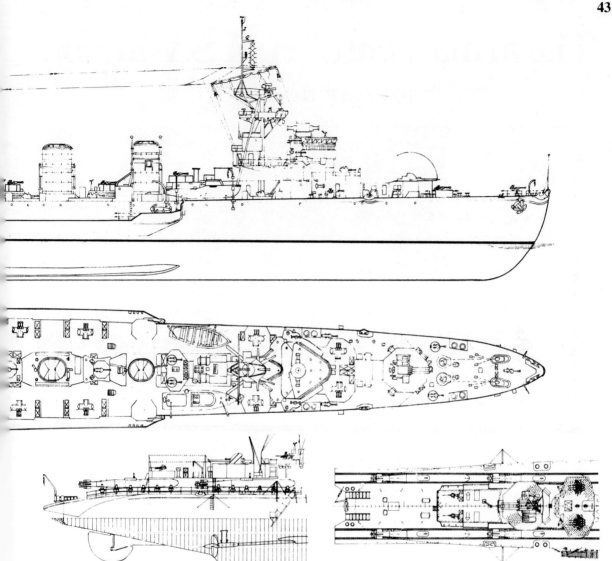

Stern of *Kitakami* showing four of her eight Kaiten. Note the special carriages to which the Kaiten have been clamped.

Author's Collection

1 April 1947. The *Kitakami* had served for more than 24 years in the IJN as CL, heavily armed torpedo cruiser, fast transport, kaiten carrier and finally repair ship under the command of SCAPJAP. A ship intended to play a major part in one of the most important stages of the decisive battle between the IJN and the USN had disappeared for ever.

[1] This may mean that as early as in 1935 it was planned to convert these ships into Torpedo Cruisers. Taking into consideration that just these ships should be converted the speculation is surely not unreasonable, but remains an idea. The official Japanese history for World War II Volume 31 *Senshi sosho Kaigun Gunsenbi Shi* part 1 deals with the conception of the Torpedo Cruiser dates from about 1936 but is also unable to give the correct date because everything was dealt with as top secret.

[2] Most sources state that the first funnel was lengthened but if we compare the rail and the searchlight platforms with the height of the funnels it seems more likely that the second and third funnels were lowered as shown in drawing no 2. The date is given according to Shizuo Fukui in his large picture book on the cruisers of the IJN from 1869 till 1945, other sources also say 1935/6.

[3] When the new BBs with 40.6cm guns appeared the elevation became greater and therefore the range longer.

[4] Shizuo Fukui deals with in his *Japanese Naval Vessels Illustrated 1869-1975, Vol 2, Cruisers, Corvettes and Sloops*, p244. Under the Shusshi Junbi Keikaku it was expected to convert five ships within three to four months at the outbreak of a war, but because of the preoccupation with the decisive encounter between the opposing forces only two ships (*Kitakami* and *Oi*) were to be converted as experimental and training cruisers. This could not be verified in other sources. The already cited official Japanese history of World War II deals with three ships only. Maybe the number of five was an unofficial plan.

[5] See footnote 1

[6] One of these mounts was somewhat altered in summer of 1943 and installed aboard Renshutei number one.

[7] *Chitose* and *Chiyoda* were converted into CVs in 1943. They needed their heavy derricks no more.

The armament of H.M.S. Warrior

by Ernest F. Slaymaker

A replica of the smooth bore muzzle-loading 68-pdr 95cwt gun on a rear chock carriage. Note the bronze sights and the firing line.

Ship's Preservation Trust

TRIALS

The armament of HMS *Warrior* was determined by a series of trials of gun versus armour. The first series was held at Woolwich in December 1856 and in April, May and June 1857. It was established that four inches of wrought-iron, whether rolled or forged, could not be penetrated by solid shot fired from the smooth-bore 68-pdr 95cwt gun with a 16lb charge at a range of 600 yards. The 68-pdr 95cwt gun was at that time the most powerful gun in the British Naval Service. When the range was reduced to 400 yards it was found that the same plate was impervious to the shot of all guns except the 68-pdr 95-cwt and even with this gun it took repeated hits on the same part of the plate to achieve penetration. The chances of hitting twice in the same place in an action at sea were very remote.

In August 1858 a trial was carried out by HMS *Excellent* at Portsmouth firing the 68-pdr 95cwt gun at 4-inch plates fitted to HMS *Alfred* and this indicated that wrought-iron plates were more resistant than either cast-iron or steel plates as then made.

In October 1858 *Excellent* carried out further trial firings against the armoured floating batteries *Erebus* and *Meteor*. These established the need for a timber backing to be fitted between the ship's side plating and her armour belt.

Influenced by the above trials the Board of Admiralty decided that HMS *Warrior* should have a 4½-inch wrought-iron armour belt with an 18-inch teak backing, and that she be armed with 40 smooth-bore 68-pdr 95cwt guns. Two of the guns were to be mounted upon the upper deck as chase guns on wooden sliding carriages on wooden pivoting and revolving slides. These carriages and slides will be dealt with in detail when describing the RBL 110-pdr 82cwt gun and its carriages. The remaining 38 guns were to be carried on the main deck, 19 a side, on wooden naval rear-chock carriages.

The Wooden Naval Rear-Chock Carriage differed from the common 'Nelsonian' truck carriage in having a rear-chock substituted for the rear axle-tree and trucks.

SMOOTH BORE 68-PDR 95CWT GUN ON WOODEN
NAVAL REAR-CHOCK CARRIAGE WITH DIRECTING
BAR OF 1861 PATTERN

Drawing by E F Slaymaker

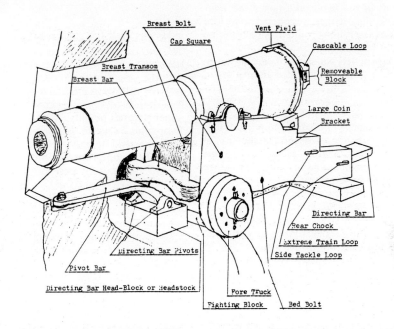

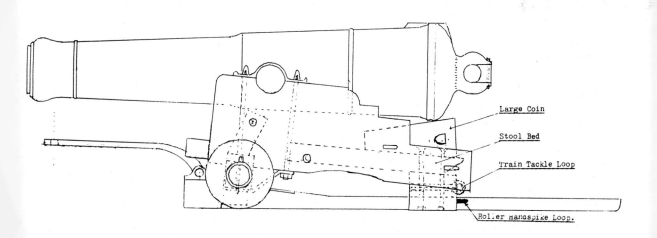

To enable these carriages to be run in and out with the same facility as a common carriage, they were provided with a loop or bracket on the rear face of the rear chock in which could be engaged the toe of a roller handspike. To run the gun in or out the roller handspikeman engaged his roller handspike in the loop, and bearing down upon the haft of the handspike raised the rear-chock from the deck; the carriage, supported on its fore trucks and the handspike rollers, could now be trundled back and forth with reasonable ease.

It was normal in wooden warships of the period to have the gun ports of sufficient width to give an arc of training of 80 to 88 degrees (40 to 44 degrees before and abaft the beam), which meant having a port some 3ft 6in wide. It was considered that *Warrior* and all future iron-clads should have the smallest possible gun ports and to achieve this it was necesssary to reduce the arc of training to 60 degrees (30 degrees either way). Some means would also have to be found to make the carriage pivot at or near the lower gun port sill.

The reduction in the arc of training was considered acceptable for the following reasons:

a The 80 to 88 degrees arc of training was a legacy of the days of sail when a ship's movements were restricted by the strength and direction of the wind.

b Steam warships rarely used such extreme training as they could use their engines to manoeuvre themselves into a favourable position to bring their guns to bear.

c Firing at extreme angles of train was neither as safe, nor could the guns be served as rapidly as when firing abeam.

To get the gun carriage to pivot at or near the gun port lower sill a Directing Bar was introduced.

THE DIRECTING BAR

The directing bar was a 'T' shaped construction of wood strengthened with iron straps, the cross of the 'T' was formed by the head block and the tail of the bar was formed by its leg. The tail of the directing bar worked in slots cut in the forward fighting block and the rear-chock of the carriage. The head block was coupled to a fighting bolt or pivot pin on the gun port lower sill by a pivot rod or bar, the whole assembly was laterally rigid and pivoted about the fighting bolt.

THE OPERATION OF THE DIRECTING BAR

When a rear-chock carriage without a directing bar was handspiked over, the rear-chock moved over and as the whole carriage pivoted at a point under the fore axle-tree, the gun muzzle was caused to swing in the opposite direction, thus precluding the use of a narrow gun port.

With the directing bar fitted the rear-chock, when moved over, carried the tail of the directing bar with it and, being laterally rigid, the rest of the directing bar also moved over, pivoting at the gun port lower sill. The head of the bar, working in the slot in the forward fighting block, carried over the fore axle-tree and trucks. As the whole assembly of gun, carriage and directing bar was now pivoting about a fighting bolt in the lower gun port sill, a port only 24-inches wide could now be used.

THE TRIAL GUN CARRIAGE

The gun carriages on the main deck of ironclads had to have a trunnion axis height that would be compatible with the height of the upper and lower gun port sills to give the following minimum requirements:

Elevation 10 degrees – governed by the trunnion axis and upper port sill heights.

Depression 7 degrees – governed by the trunnion axis and lower port sill heights.

Arc of Training 60 degrees – governed by the diameter of the gun barrel at the gun port when the gun is run out.

When 'housed' the flat face of the gun muzzle was to overlap the upper port sill by at least two inches. This would be governed by the trunnion axis, the thickness of the rear-chock, the thickness of the housing bed, and the upper port sill height. The housing bed was used where the overlap of the gun muzzle would be too great.

A trial rear-chock carriage and directing bar was manufactured by the Royal Carriage Department and sent to HMS *Excellent*, one of whose ports had been suitably modified to receive it. The modified gun port had the following dimensions:

Upper port sill 64in above the deck.

Lower port sill 18in high.

Width 24in.

The carriage differed from the one that was finally adopted in the following respects:

a The trunnion axis was 33½ inches above the deck.

b The gun port would admit of 15 degrees elevation and 7 degrees depression.

c The maximum elevation that the carriage would allow was 15 degrees and this was with the base ring of the gun resting upon the rear-chock. At this elevation the gun muzzle would clear the upper port sill and the gun could not be housed in the normal manner.

d To obtain the 15 degrees elevation the rear-chock was about four inches thinner than was normal.

e Because the rear-chock was thin, the train tackle loop could not be placed upon the centre-line, so it was placed alongside the directing bar slot.

f The directing bar head-block was lower and narrower.

g A single pivot bar or rod was used.

h The breast bar on the carriage was lower.

On 15 December 1860 firing trials were carried out in HMS *Excellent* and the reports on these trials were received at the Admiralty on 21 December. Copies of them are held in the Public Records Office.

The reports said that the carriage was too low and recommended raising the lower gun port sill by four inches to 22 inches and of course the trunnion axis of the carriage a similar amount to 37½ inches. With this alteration the depression that the port would allow remained at 7 degrees, but the elevation was reduced to 12

**AN IMPRESSION OF THE DIRECTING BAR WITH THE
STRONGER PIVOTING BAR THAT WAS FIRST USED
WITH THE MAIN DECK GUN CARRIAGES IN HMS
WARRIOR**

Drawing by E F Slaymaker

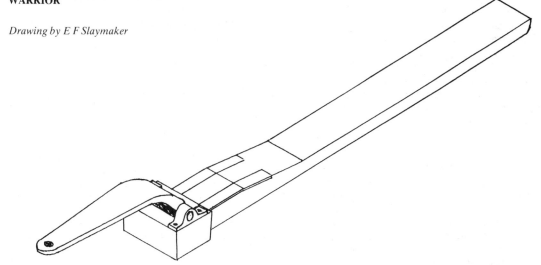

WOODEN NAVAL REAR-CHOCK CARRIAGE FOR SMOOTH BORE 68-PDR 95CWT GUN

With slots in the fighting block and the rear-chock for the directing bar.

Drawing by E F Slaymaker

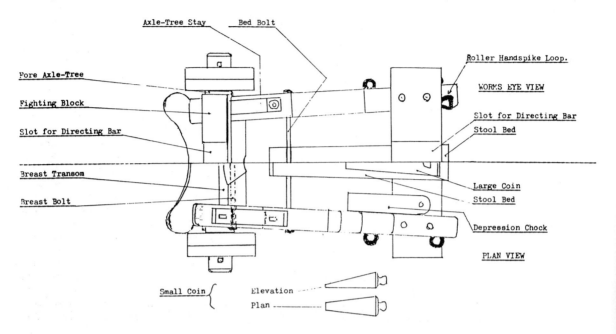

degrees. Although this would give a reduction in range from 3620 yards to 3200 yards it was considered acceptable. Firing trials by HMS *Excellent* had demonstrated that a well-trained gun crew, when firing a 68-pdr gun to a range of 3000 yards at a target the size of a line of battleships, could only be expected to hit it with 11 to 12 per cent of the shots fired. Considering that this was from a stationary ship with no motion to a stationary target, it will be seen that there was little chance of hitting above 3000 yards from a rolling ship. The trials also revealed that the directing bar pivot rod was weak; this was remedied by fitting the improved and stronger pivoting bar shown in figures 1–3.

The recommendations were ordered to be adopted forthwith, just eight days before the *Warrior* was launched.

CHANGES IN ARMAMENT

Meanwhile the first change in the ship's armament had been authorised. On 25 September 1860 four of the main deck 68-pdrs (probably the two foremost and the two aftermost) were ordered to be removed and replaced by four of the new Armstrong rifled breech loading 40-pdr 32cwt guns mounted on the upper deck. Then on 28 February 1861, the upper deck chase guns were ordered to be replaced by two Armstrong rifled breech loading 110-pdr 82cwt guns (then called 100-pdrs) on sliding carriages and pivoting and revolving slides.

On 22 August 1861, eight RBL 110-pdr 82cwt guns were taken aboard, replacing the same number of 68-pdrs in the main deck battery.

When *Warrior* sailed for Portsmouth on 19 September 1861 her armament was:

26 SB 68-pdr 95cwt guns on rear-chock carriages with directing bars on the main deck.

10 RBL 110-pdr 82cwt guns; two on sliding carriages and slides as chase guns on the upper deck, eight on rear-chock carriages with directing bars on the main deck.

4 RBL 40-pdr 32cwt guns on common wooden naval carriages on the upper deck.

2 RBL 20-pdr 13cwt guns for the two 42ft launches, a field marine carriage and limber was carried for each of these guns.

1 RBL 12-pdr 8cwt gun for the 32ft pinnace, a field marine carriage and limber was also carried for this gun.

1 SB 6-pdr 6cwt brass gun on a wooden elevating carriage for short range practice.

It will be observed that although pierced for 38 guns on the main deck only 34 guns were actually mounted. As completed *Warrior* was found to trim by the head, and it was probably as partial compensation that it was arranged that the four empty main deck gun ports should be the foremost ones, and that the 40-pdrs were normally mounted aft on the upper deck.

The main deck guns were disposed as follows:

Gun Ports (Port and Starboard)	Gun Nos (Port and Starboard)	
1st and 2nd	Nil	
3rd and 4th	Nos 1 and 2	(110-pdrs)
5th to 15th	Nos 3 to 13	(68-pdrs)
16th and 17th	Nos 14 and 15	(110-pdrs)
18th and 19th	Nos 16 and 17	(68-pdrs)

On 15 November 1861 the Admiralty directed that the upper deck 40-pdrs should be replaced by an equal number of RBL 70-pdr 60cwt guns when available. The 70-pdr failed its proof tests and was never issued so the 40-pdr 32cwt guns remained until about November 1863 when they were replaced by RBL 40-pdr 35cwt guns.

By the early part of 1863 firing practices at sea revealed that the single pivot bar fitted to the directing bar was unsatisfactory so an improved one with a raised head-block of greater width, widely spaced pivots, and two pivot bars was introduced. The breast bar of the carriage was raised so as to rest neatly upon the directing bar head block pivots when the gun was in the 'run-out' position (figures 5–7).

In 1863 one or more of the main deck guns were mounted upon wooden sliding carriages on wooden naval broadside slides. They were the same as those used for the upper deck 110-pdrs except that they were fitted with a raised head-block and two pivot bars to pivot on the port sill pivot bolt. Captain Cochrane rendered his

report upon them in October 1863. By January 1864 a part of the main deck armament was upon sliding carriages and slides, the rest still upon rear-chock carriages with directing bars.

THE SMOOTH-BORE 68-pdr 95cwt GUN ON ITS WOODEN NAVAL REAR-CHOCK CARRIAGE WITH DIRECTING BAR (Figures 1, 2, 5 and 6)

The largest of the *Warrior*'s guns both in calibre and weight was the cast-iron smooth bore 68-pdr 95cwt gun, to which the following data applies:

Cast-iron with a nominal weight of 96cwt
Preponderance (breech heaviness): $10\frac{1}{2}$ cwt

Length: Nominal (face of muzzle to base ring) 120in. Overall 135.55in

Diameters: at the base ring 27.76in; over the muzzle swell 18.65in; of trunnions 8.12in (the trunnions were underhung 2in)

Width: Shoulder to shoulder between the trunnions 23.68in. Outside the trunnions 36.68in

Bore: Smooth, 8.12in in diameter with a length of 113.9in. The vent entered the bore at a point 2.5in from the bottom (111.4in from the muzzle)

The gun was supplied with spherical shot and shell, cylindrical case shot, and grape shot. The solid shot had a diameter of 7.849 to 7.925in and a nominal weight of 68lbs. The actual weight varied as follows: cast-iron shot 67lb, chilled iron shot $69\frac{1}{2}$lbs, wrought iron shot 72lbs.

SMOOTH BORE 68-PDR 95CWT GUN ON WOODEN NAVAL REAR-CHOCK CARRIAGE WITH DIRECTING BAR (Circa 1863)

Drawing by E F Slaymaker

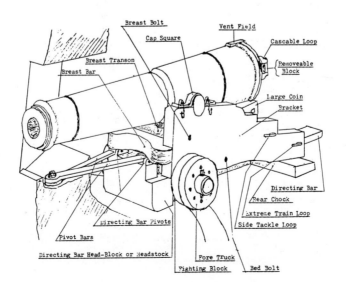

Red hot shot could be fired by heating cast-iron shot in the ship's furnaces and then transporting them to the guns in special iron shot bearers. These missiles would be particularly effective against wooden ships. Cylindrical case shot had sheet iron cases 7.82in in diameter with plate iron tops and bottoms to which were attached iron handles, they were filled with 90 8oz balls and weight 50½lbs filled. When case shot were fired from the gun, the discharge broke up the case and the shattered remains with the balls left the muzzle and spread in a similar manner to the shot from a shot-gun.

The pattern of grape shot in use in 1860 was known as 'Tiered Grapeshot' or 'Caffin's Grape-shot', those for the 68-pdr gun consisted of 15 3lb iron balls placed in three tiers, separated by iron discs 7.4in in diameter and 0.55in thick and secured by an iron pin. When fired from the gun, the discs and pin broke up allowing the balls to spread on leaving the muzzle. Owing to the greater weight of the balls grape-shot ranged further than case-shot.

The following types of shell were used:

Common shell were hollow spheres with a diameter of 7.925in containing a bursting charge of 2lb 9oz of gunpowder and a time fuze. Their weight filled was 49lbs 10oz.

Filled diaphragm shrapnel shell, contained 341 balls, a 5oz bursting charge and a time fuze. Their weight filled was 60lb 13oz. The balls were separated from the gunpowder bursting charge by a metal diaphragm.

Both of the above shells were fitted with wooden bottoms to prevent them rolling in the bore and to keep the fuze facing the muzzle. If the shell was allowed to roll in the bore, the protruding fuze would cause it to jam in the barrel of the gun with disastrous results. The bottoms of sea service shells had a hole in the middle; this allowed metal to metal contact when a gun was double shotted with a shell on top of a shot.

Martin's Molten Iron Shell were hollow iron spheres filled with molten iron. The wall of the shell was thinner than that of a common shell, but was made thicker at the bottom to take the shock of firing. When the shell struck, it broke up and the molten iron ignited any woodwork or combustible material with which it came in contact. A cupola furnace was required to melt the iron filling. The shells were not fired until at least four minutes had elapsed since pouring in the molten iron, and they were still effective an hour after filling. Martin's shell were introduced in 1860 to replace red hot shot, being safer to handle, load and fire, as well as being more effective.

Details of the 8in Martin's shell, which was used by both the 68-pdr and the SB 8-in guns:

Wall thickness: at bottom 1in, at sides 0.5in. The inside was coated with a 0.25in coating of moulding loam.

Diameter: 7.86in empty, 7.875in filled (the projectile expanded with the heat after filling).

Filling hole: 1.2in in diameter.

Weight empty (including the loam lining and the wooden bottom): 33lbs.

Weight of molten iron to fill the shell: 26lbs.

Weight of shell filled: 59lbs.

Carcasses: These were hollow iron spheres filled with combustible materials. They had two or more fire holes in them to enable the flame of the guns discharge to ignite the contents.

The flannel covered gunpowder charges were of three sizes:

Distant   16lbs, 7.55in in diameter and 11.5in long.
Full   12lbs, 7.5in in diameter and 9.5in long.
Reduced   8lbs, 7.3in in diameter and 7.4in long.

The 16lb charge could only be used with solid shot and common shell, for all other projectiles the maximum charge was 12lb. The charges were conveyed from the magazine to the guns in leather cases 8.9in in diameter, 17in long and weighing 6lb 6oz empty.

With a solid shot and a 16lb charge, the gun had a muzzle velocity of 1579ft/sec and ranged to 3200 yards at 12 degrees elevation with a time of flight of 12.875 seconds. With a solid shot and a 12lb charge, the gun ranged to 3070 yards at 12 degrees elevation.

With a common shell and a 16lb charge, the gun had a muzzle velocity of 1809ft/sec and ranged to 3100 yards at 12 degrees elevation.

With a common shell and a 12lb charge, the gun ranged to 2990 yards at 12 degrees elevation.

THE WOODEN NAVAL REAR-CHOCK CARRIAGE AND DIRECTING BAR FOR SMOOTH-BORE 68-pdr GUNS OF 95cwt (Figures 1 to 7)

All 26 of the *Warrior's* 68-pdrs were carried on the Main Deck on Wooden Naval Rear-Chock Carriages with Directing Bars. The carriages differed from the normal rear-chock carriages in that they were modified for use with a directing bar. This entailed cutting slots in the forward fighting block and the rear-chock for the bar to work in, and in fitting a breast bar across the front of the carriage. Provision was also made for an elevating screw in addition to the normal coin. The third step down at the rear of the carriage brackets was omitted in order to provide clearance for the elevating handle. Elevating screws were ordered to be fitted to all smooth-bore gun carriages in 1862.

The data applicable to the carriage were as follows:

Weight: 13½cwt

Length excluding breast bar: 77½in

Trunnion axles: 37½in above the deck

Diameter of trucks: 20in

Maximum elevation that the carriage would admit: 16½ degrees (stool bed removed and the base ring on the rear-chock).

Elevation for housing: 14 degrees (stool bed removed, housing bed installed with the base ring resting upon it).

Maximum elevation with the stool bed installed: 12 degrees.

Maximum elevation with the depression chock swung back under the stool bed: approximately 1 degree.

With the stool bed installed, the use of the large coin gave from 1½ degrees depression to 7 degrees elevation and use of the small coin gave from 6 to 11 degrees of elevation. With the depression chock swung back under the stool bed, use of the large coin gave from 7 degrees depression to 1 degree elevation.

**SMOOTH BORE 68-PDR 95cwt GUN ON WOODEN NAVAL
REAR-CHOCK CARRIAGE WITH DIRECTING BAR**

Drawing by E F Slaymaker

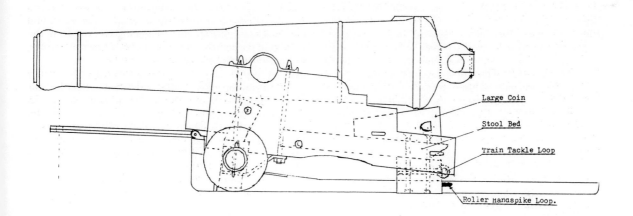

Large Coin

Stool Bed

Train Tackle Loop

Roller Handspike Loop.

**DIRECTING BAR FOR THE REAR CHOCK CARRIAGES
OF THE S.B. 68-PDR 95CWT AND RBL 7IN 82CWT GUNS**
Note: the RBL 7in gun was formerly called the Armstrong
110-pdr gun.

Drawing by E F Slaymaker

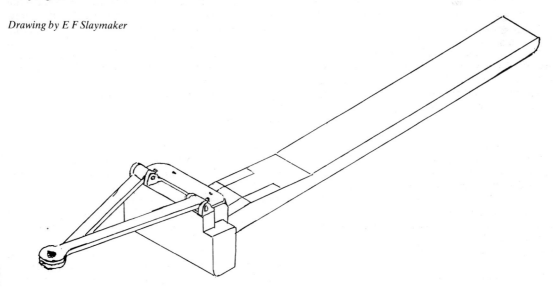

The elevating screw, when fitted, gave the following approximate elevations:

Elevating screw installed in the rear-chock: 4 to 12 degrees elevation.

Elevating screw installed in the stool bed: $2\frac{1}{2}$ degrees depression to $5\frac{1}{2}$ degrees elevation.

Elevating screw in stool bed and depression chock swung back under: 1 to 8 degrees depression.

The gun ports had the lower port sill at 22 inches, and the upper at 64 inches above the waterway. The port would admit 12 degrees elevation and 7 degrees depression.

The recoil of the gun and carriage was limited by a 9-inch hawser-laid breeching passed through the cascable loop and secured to $1\frac{5}{8}$-inch breeching bolts on each side of the gun port. Additional bolts of the same size were provided for a preventer breeching. The breeching was adjusted to bring the gun muzzle 12 to 18 inches inboard of the inner port sill when the gun was fully in. The gun was run out after loading by side tackles, the moving blocks of which were hooked to the side tackle loops on the carriage brackets, and the hauling blocks, to the $1\frac{1}{2}$ inch side tackle bolts either side of the gun port. A train tackle was supplied to run the gun in, its hauling blocks being hooked to the train tackle loop on the rear face of the rear-chock, and the standing block to the train tackle deck bolt set 15ft inboard of the inner port sill. The side tackles and train tackle, collectively known as gun tackles, were of 3-inch hemp rove through 10-inch double blocks. The blocks had $3\frac{1}{2}$-inch hemp strops but these were later replaced by 2-inch wire rope.

THE DIRECTING BAR IN ITS FINAL FORM (CIRCA 1863)

Weighed about 5cwt. The head block was $29\frac{1}{2}$in wide and crowned by the hinges for the two pivot bars. The height of the head block was governed by the need for the pivot bar hinges to fit snugly under the breast bar when the gun was fully out. The tail of the bar was 12-13in wide and of sufficient length to remain engaged in the slot in the rear-chock when the gun was fully in.

Behind the head block, the tail of the directing bar was raised to a height sufficient to raise the fore axle-tree and take the weight of the carriage off its trucks.

An iron sweep plate or racer was fitted under the head block to enable it to be traversed more easily and to prevent the trucks from digging into the deck.

The rear-chock carriage with directing bar was not an unqualified success, it required considerable effort to traverse the gun and carriage. When firing a lee gun with considerable heel on the ship, it was found that the gun would often run out again before the slack of the train tackle could be taken up. This caused the carriage to come up with a bang against the head block of the directing bar, the shock being transmitted through the pivot bars would cause the fighting bolt or pivot to shear. Another problem was the five minutes taken to cast loose the gun when clearing for action.

Most of the time was taken in raising the base ring of the gun from the 'housed' position which required the utmost efforts of five and sometimes six men, instead of the normal four men with two handspikes. With ordinary common and rear-chock carriages, any minor adjustments to the gun's training could be managed by one man with a handspike, but this proved impossible with the directing bar fitted.

The situation was improved when rollers were fitted to the directing bar head block in 1864. The final solution was to adapt the upper deck sliding carriage and slide to broadside use by giving it a raised head block with pivots and pivot bars, pivoting on a strengthened pivot bolt at the gun port lower will.

To be continued.

BRITISH NAVAL GUNS 1880~1945
by N J M Campbell

4 INCH GUNS

In view of the number of Marks, BL and QFC guns are considered separately from QF.

4in BL/13cwt Mark I These guns, of which 19 were made, were not numbered in the main 4in series. They were 14.8cals and fired a 25lb shell at 1180f/s. They were built with a steel A tube, wrought iron jacket, trunnions and B coil and were not chase-hooped. Cup obturation was fitted with a radial vent. It was intended that the *Inflexible* should have six, but they do not seem to have been mounted and the gun was in a few minor vessels only. They were withdrawn after the accident in 1891 to a 6in BL MK II in *Cordelia*. Mountings were RCDI ($+12° - 8°$) or VBII ($+20° - 30°$) and range 5500yds/20°.

4in BL Mark I This was similar to the above but was 25cals and 22½cwt with MV 1790f/s. Only eight guns were mounted in the *Swiftsure* though 27 were made and were withdrawn after the *Cordelia* accident. The mountings were VBI ($+18½° - 28°$) giving a stated range of 7200yds.

4in BL Marks II to VI All were steel trunnioned guns differing in details of construction with de Bange obturation and axial vents, and were 27cals with weights of 22-27cwt. In all 53 MK II, 20 MK III, 67 MK IV, 106 MK V, 61 MK VI were made but 11 MK V and 40 MK VI were land service, largely in India. They were for field defences on over-bank carriages and not for coast defence, though latterly various marks were used as drill guns. They must not be confused with the 30-pdr field gun, also a 4in/27cal and only used in India. MK II was not chase-hooped while IIP differed in having percussion instead of friction firing. MK III originally not chase-hooped, was rebuilt as IIIA with a B tube in front of the original B hoop to the muzzle. MK IV had a heavier A tube and remained without chase-hooping, while MK V was built with a row of four chase hoops and MK VI with a B tube as in IIIA. All had three motion BM.

They were mounted in many of the old battleships with RMLs including *Inflexible* which had eight, and otherwise mainly in gunboats and the first from torpedo-gunboats. Mountings were VBII in battleships and a few gunboats with VBI retained in *Swiftsure*, and otherwise VCPI ($+20° - 20°$ or $-14°$).

4in QFC A maximum of 27 guns and possibly only 20, were converted from BL Mks IIIA, IV, V, VI and known as QFC Mk I/IIIA etc. They were either given new A tubes or short bore and chamber liners with chambers as in 4in QF Mk I to III. They replaced BL guns in the *Inflexible*, the first from TGB and the gunboat *Lapwing*. In the 1914-1918 war a few were in DAMS and possibly the auxiliary patrol while three were used by Belgian forces on Lake Tanganyika. Mountings were VBIIC or VCPIC, both 20° elevation. Separate ammunition was used.

4in BL Mark VII In all 600 of these 50.3cal guns were made, the typical Mk VII being built with inner A and A tubes, wire for 108.65in and B tube to muzzle with jacket, breech ring and breech bush screwed into the A tube. The Welin block had 'pure couple' BM so that the guns were originally called A Mk VII. Mk VII covered two early guns used for proof and experimental purposes with a modified breech block, and Mk VII** one gun designed by Beardmore only differing in details of constructional dimensions. Mk VII*** comprised 15 guns with no inner A and B and jacket combined in one, and Mk VII one Vickers stock gun with radial instead of parallel keyways on the breech ring and needing a special cradle. The Mk VII was mounted in dreadnoughts from the 'Bellerophon' class to the 'King George V' class and in battlecruisers from the *Indefatigable* to the *Queen Mary* as secondary armament as well as in the *Indomitable* from April 1917. It was also in the 'Boadicea', 'Active' and 'Bristol' class light cruisers and in some First World War P boats, sloops, armed boarding steamers, Q ships, DAMS and one trawler while the British forces on Lake Tanganyika also had one. In World War II it was mostly in DEMS. Mountings were PII, II$_x$, IV, IV$_x$, IV$_{xx}$, VI, VIII allowing 15° elevation or 15¼° in PII, XX$_x$.

There were a few used as coast defence guns in 1914/1918 including at least one on a naval field mounting, and in World War II it was widely used in emergency coast defence batteries while 20 were mounted on lorries as 'field' artillery.

In the latter part of the First World War it was also used as a naval AA gun on 60° HA Mk II mountings firing a reduced charge. At the end of 1918 these were in -2 guns; *Bellerophon, Temeraire, Princess Royal:* 1 gun; *Centurion, Monarch, Orion, Colossus, Australia, New Zealand, Indomitable, Inflexible, Bellona, Blanche, Blonde.* One was mounted on the N Foreland, largely as a star shell gun.

54

Drawing of the 4in BL Mar IX gun in CPI mounting by John Lambert. Reproduced from *Naval Weapons of World War Two* by N J M Campbell.

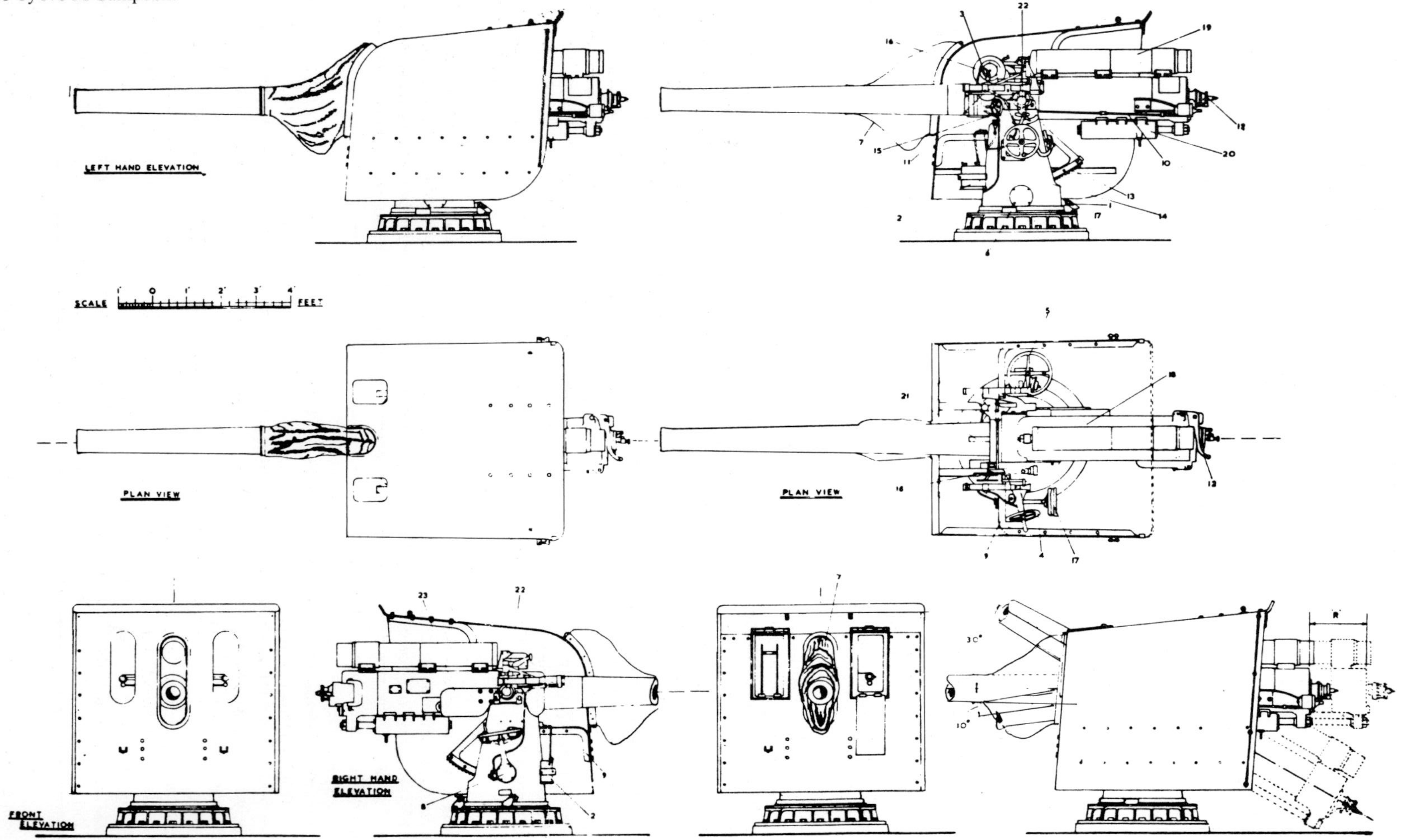

LEFT HAND ELEVATION

PLAN VIEW

SCALE |— FEET

PLAN VIEW

RIGHT HAND ELEVATION

FRONT ELEVATION

1 Training stop
2 Battery box
3 Dial lamp
4 Elevating handwheel

5 Training handwheel
6 Access plate to elevating gear
7 Canvas ballast bag
8 Access plate to training gear

9 Bracket for supporting shield
10 Firing pull rod
11 Telescope holder
12 Bench mechanism lever

13 Elevating arc
14 Pedestal
15 Range handwheel
16 Range dial

17 Body rest
18 Cradle
19 Spring case
20 Recoil cylinder

21 Gun key
22 Trunnion cap
23 Body shield
John Lambert

	4in BL IIIA-VI	4in QFC	4in BL MkVII	4in BL MkVIII, XI	4in BL Mk IX
Weight incl BM (tons)	1.30/1.35	1.30	2.092	1.296 (XI 1.304)	2.125
Length oa (in)	120	120	208.45	166.4	184.6
Length bore (cals)	27	27.78	50.31	39.8	44.35
Chamber (cu in)	417	212.5	600	298	470.3
Chamber length (in)	18.5	14.4	27.75	15.92	25.493
Projectile (lb)	25	25	31	31	31
Charge (lb/Type)	12 SP	3.56 Cord 15	9.37 MD 16	5.38 MD 16	7.69 MD 16
	3.06 Cord 5		9.69 SC 103	5.54 SC 103	7.914 SC 103
Muzzle Velocity (f/s)	1900 SP	2192	2864	2287	2642
	1903 Cord				
Range (yds)	7700/20°	9000/20°	11,600/15°	10,210/20°	13,840/30°

On HA (60°) mountings BL Mk VII had a 6.04lb MD8 charge and MV *c* 2400 f/s. BL Mk IX also fired a 9.39lb NF/S 164-048 charge with unaltered MV.

4in BL Mark VIII Two hundred and forty-six of these 39.8cal guns were made, the original construction comprising A tube, breech piece and B tube to muzzle, wire over breech piece, jacket, breech ring and bush screwed into breech piece. A Welin block was used with 'pure couple' BM so that they were originally called A Mk VIII. When worn a taper liner was inserted and the last 28 guns had a tapered inner A and A tube instead of the A tube, B tube and breech piece. Mk VIIIx covered the first six guns with a different shape of chamber and breech ring and modified breech block. The Mk VIII was mounted in the first 4in destroyers from the later 'Tribals' to the first 13 of the K class. It was also in the *Swift*, the Australian 'Swan' class, a few P boats, the 'Fly' class river gunboats and some Q ships as well as the submarines *E2, E11, E12, E14, E21, E25*. One gun is recorded in the Japanese destroyer *Sakaki* in 1918 and four went to the Caspian in 1919. The Mk VIII was also used in DEMS in World War II.

Mountings were PIII, IIIx, IIIxx, V, VII, all with 20° elevation, with a few 'Trap-door' HA conversions, recorded in the K class, *Acasta, Midge, Spitfire* (one).

4in BL Mark IX This 44.35cal gun was a BL version of the QF Mk V, introduced for electric director firing in the secondary batteries of the 'Renown' class. It was a widely used gun and 2382 were made. As Mk IXx there was an A tube, taper wound wire to the muzzle, full length jacket, breech ring and bush screwed into the A tube with Welin block and single motion BM. On lining with a tapered inner A it became Mk IX and some guns were originally built in this way. Mk IXxx was introduced to suit old plant at EOC and COW, and had step wound wire with B tube and shorter jacket. There was no inner A and when this was fitted it became Mk IXxxx. Mk IXxxx covered 50 guns with the start of the breech block thread 180° out of position, needing special breech bushes. The gun was in triple mountings in the 'Renown' and 'Courageous' classes and in single mountings in the 'Renown' class also, as well as in the *Inflexible* from July 1917, the *Topaze* as re-armed and the monitors *Erebus, Terror, Marshal Soult, Lord Clive* and *Sir John Moore*. M27 had a triple mounting fitted in 1919, while single mountings were in World War I sloops, minesweepers, 'Kil' gunboats, many auxiliary warships and DAMS. In World War II they were chiefly in 'Flower' class corvettes, Australian minesweepers, auxiliaries of many types and DEMS.

The Mk I Triple mounting, the single PXV and much more common CPI allowed 30° elevation while the PXII limited to the 'Renown' class had 25°.

Some were used as emergency coast defence guns in World War II, including two on South Georgia, and also as fixed and lorry born 'field' artillery with 25 of the latter guns.

4in BL Mark X Originally for the Norwegian 'Nidaros' class taken over as the *Gorgon* and *Glatton*, this EOC Pattern T was in British service a 45cal gun of partly wire wound type with coned breech block and ballistics as for the Mk IX. Fifteen guns were made and it was only in DAMS in PXIV mountings allowing 20° elevation.

4in BL Mark XI This gun was a Mk VIII adapted for the cradle of the SI submarine mounting. It was of the later construction with tapered inner A and A tube. 30 guns were made and are recorded for *J1, K1-4, K6-16*. The balance and those removed from rearmed submarines, were in Q ships. The SI mounting allowed 20° elevation.

4in BL Mark XII Similar to an unwired Mk VII, this 50.3cal gun was a Vickers Mk E introduced to the Spanish navy in November 1909. Twenty guns were delivered to Britain in 1917/18 but were never mounted afloat. MV was 2824f/s with a 31lb shell.

4in BL Mark XIII EOC Pattern U, a 39.9cal gun similar to Mk VIIIx but with a different BM. Four guns intended for the Brazilian submarine depot ship *Ceara* were acquired in 1918 but never mounted afloat.

4in BL Mark XIV EOC Pattern H, a 50cal 43cwt gun built for the 1906 Milan Exhibition, and in stock at Pozzuoli at the end of 1913. The gun was partly wire wound and had a three-piece A tube and coned breech block. EOC figures give the MV as 2516f/s with 31lb shell. The only gun was mounted in the Portuguese transport *India* (ex Austrian *Vorwaertz*) in February 1918.

A design for a 4in BL with the contours of the Mk VIII and MV 1575f/s was approved on 28 February 1940, but was supplanted by the WF Mk XIX.

Maintenance of post-war British sea-power

by P G Pugh BSc, MRAeS CEng

In common with all modern fleets, the size and form of the Royal Navy has been forced between the hammer of ever-rising unit costs and the anvil of national budgets. The annual publication of the 'Statement on the Defence Estimates' – often known as the UK Defence White Papers – has charted this process in an annual outpouring of statistics. These are reviewed in this article to illustrate the evolution of the Royal Navy over the last four decades with particular emphasis on the effects of the continuous rise in unit costs outlined by the author in his earlier article ('Of ships and money: the rising cost of naval power', *Warship* 32).

THE MYTH OF THE DECLINING BUDGET

There is a persistent myth that contraction of the Royal Navy has been due to paucity of funding compared to that which it enjoyed in its hey-day. In fact, the long-term trend has been one of growing expenditure which, in recent years, has reached historically high levels for peacetime even after allowing for inflation. Current levels of defence spending average around five per cent of the Gross National Product (GNP) which is considerably higher than the two per cent to four per cent share of much smaller GNP figures allotted to defence during periods of peace between the end of the War of the Spanish Succession in 1713 and the rearmament in the late 1930s. Thus, in the middle of the nineteenth century the dominance of the Pax Britannica was maintained on Naval Estimates of around £6m or the equivalent of about £67m in terms of retail purchasing power in 1975 ie *circa* five per cent only of the money actually spent on the Royal Navy in that year. Again, in real terms (after allowing for inflation) the total UK defence budget in 1913, at the height of the dreadnought race prior to the First World War, was but 61 per cent of the expenditure on the Royal Navy alone in 1975.

Such differences in expenditure are inevitably reflected in the value of the active fleet. Approximate calculations based on cost trends described in the earlier article by the author and presented in Fig 1 show the replacement cost of the Royal Navy in 1982 to have been very similar to that during 1940 and to well exceed the corresponding figures for 1814 and 1914.

Turning to more recent times, Fig 2 shows expenditure on the Royal Navy expressed in real terms from 1946 to 1984. Far from a consistently declining expenditure, the underlying trend has been one of increased spending with the purchasing power of the funding provided growing, on average, at about 2 per cent per annum.

Thus, the idea that declining budgets were responsible for the financial pressures felt by the Royal Navy is contrary to the facts. The pressures have been real enough; but they arose despite a rising budget. Their true cause was that while budgets rose unit costs rose even faster.

It is pertinent to note that neither of the two major post-war reappraisals of the roles of the Royal Navy (around 1965 and 1981) correspond to any marked reduction in funding or other interruption of the general trend. They should not be seen as isolated convulsions in policy. Rather, they were but instances when the procurement cycles of particular types of ship brought the continuous problem of rising unit costs into especially sharp focus.

GROWTH OF UNIT COSTS & ITS PRESSURE ON BUDGETS

The costs of buying new vessels attract most public attention. These are unambiguously attributable to each individual warship, first signal each round of cost increases and are the most immediate obstacle to any replacement of outdated ships. However, they are far from being the largest item in the annual budget – which has to cover all the costs of all the vessels in the fleet each at various stages in their service lives. A typical breakdown of the annual cost of a modern navy is given in Fig 3 which shows that indirect costs (infrastructure etc) are of broadly the same size as the direct costs – ie costs attributable to individual ships. Within the latter, the ownership element (running and refit costs) predominates.

However, acquisition and ownership costs are both driven by increasing size and complexity in much the same way so that they remain roughly in step and trends in production cost are a fair guide to trends in the total of all direct costs. Similar arguments may be extended to indirect costs, for it is reasonable to suppose that the size of the infrastructure should vary in sympathy with the size and complexity of the operations that it supports.

This is not to say that every element of cost is inevitably tied to a precise proportionality to production cost. Indeed, it is not difficult to adduce examples to the contrary from particular features of the designs of individual ships. However, we are concerned here with trends in the cost of a fleet. This is the aggregate of many different cost elements – some varying faster and some slower than in proportion to production costs. So, while recognising that it is a significant assumption, we are justified in this context in using production costs as a surrogate for total costs when averaged across a whole class of ships or for the entire fleet.

Fig. 1: Replacement costs of Royal Navy

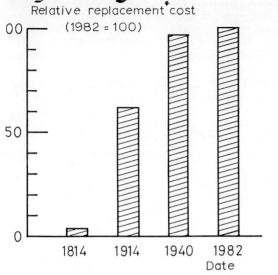

Relative replacement*cost
(1982 = 100)
00
50
0
1814
1914
1940
1982
Date

*Replacement by ships of average contemporary standards on one-for-one basis

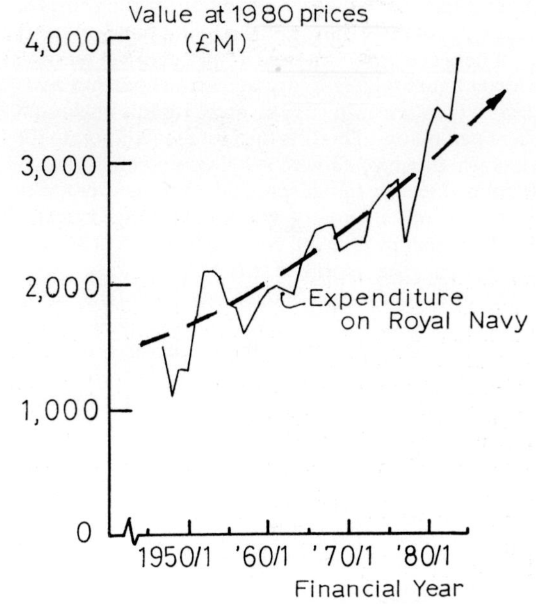

Value at 1980 prices
(£M)
4,000
3,000
2,000
1,000
0
Expenditure on Royal Navy
1950/1
'60/1
'70/1
'80/1
Financial Year

Data from Defence White Papers & corrected for inflation using R.P.I.. Indirect costs attribute pro-rata to direct costs.

Fig. 2: Spending on Royal Navy

TOTAL ANNUAL COST
Indirect
Direct
Source : 1984 UK Defence White Paper
DIRECT COSTS
(L.C.C. Analysis)
Production
Other initial costs
Running
Refits
Source : Andrews & Brown, ASNAME 1980

Fig. 3: Production costs & annual expenditure

R.N. active fleet: submarines, frigates & larger vessels
No. of ships
150
100
50
0
2½% p.a. contraction
Financial Year
1950/1
60/1
70/1
80/1

Fig. 4: R.N. Numerical Strength

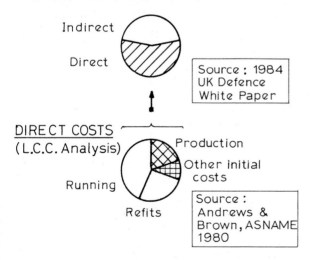

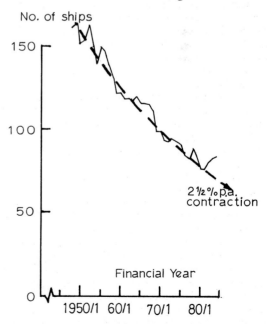

Other studies have shown that unit production costs of various types of vessel have risen at (compound interest) rates of between 3 per cent and 13 per cent per annum. The lower figure relates to aircraft carriers but unit costs of aircraft themselves have risen more rapidly at about 8 per cent per annum. This lifts the cost escalation rate for carriers when equipped with a full complement of aircraft (plus reserves, initial spares etc.) to near equality with that for other types of warship. Averaged over a typical fleet, unit production costs have grown at around 9 per cent pa since World War II.

Thus, while the naval budget has increased, upon average, at 2 per cent pa the cost of an up-to-date ship of given type (carrier, destroyer, frigate or whatever) has increased at about 9 per cent per annum. Therefore, the cost of keeping a fleet of constant size and formation fully up to date has continually outrun the money available by some 7 per cent per annum. Since a 7 per cent per annum increase compounds up into a doubling (money available only half that required) in each decade, it is little wonder that financial constraints have been ever present and defence policy reviews have been a regular feature of the post-war experience of the Royal Navy as for all major navies.

LIVING WITH COST GROWTH
With unit costs rising so much faster than the budget, something had to give. To find out what this was we first examine all the broad policy options theoretically available and identify which of these was adopted in practice. The next section of this essay then sees how this broad policy was worked out in the number and types of ships of the Royal Navy.

The most obvious option – which was taken to a considerable degree – is a reduction in the size of the fleet. As shown in Fig 4, the size of the active fleet (measured by the number of vessels of frigate or fleet submarine size or larger) declined at a long-term average rate of about $2\frac{1}{2}$ per cent per annum. This, together with the 2 per cent per annum growth in total expenditure, means that the average annual cost per vessel increased at circa $4\frac{1}{2}$ per cent per annum. If this is now compared with the 9 per cent per annum growth in the unit costs of up-to-date ships (of any given type), it will be seen that savings of $4\frac{1}{4}$ per cent per annum have been made year-upon-year by means other than the simple reduction in the number of ships.

In theory this saving might have been made by failing to keep the fleet up to date in terms of the performance and equipment of the various types of warship. This could have been done by designing new vessels to less demanding requirements than their foreign contemporaries. However, comparison of post-war UK and foreign vessels shows no evidence of the large divergence between unit production costs of similar types of ship – a halving of UK unit costs relative to contemporary foreign products every 16 years – that would have been necessary upon such a policy. Alternatively, a similar overall saving could have been achieved by increasing the average service life of RN ships so that they, and their costs, fell back steadily relative to contemporary standards of the best. While some ships have

had remarkably long service lives they have usually been updated during refits and service lives have certainly not increased to the extent – an increase of 15 years between, say, 1950 and 1980 – which would have been necessary to save on cost at $4\frac{1}{4}$ per cent per annum over all that period by such means. Yet more convincingly, the performance of the Royal Navy during 1982 in the South Atlantic refutes any suggestion that the overall quality of its equipment had been allowed to fall behind the best standards of the day.

The $4\frac{1}{4}$ per cent per annum additional savings were actually made via changes in the formation of the fleet ie in the balance of relative numbers of different types of warship. Costs were reduced by a progressive shift towards the smaller (and cheaper) types of ship while keeping these fully up to date. Around 1980, a fleet aircraft carrier, even without its aircraft, cost some 50 times as much as a frigate so there is ample scope for cost reduction by this means. The arithmetic of adapting to cost escalation was, thus, as summarised in Table 1.

TABLE 1: THE ARITHEMETIC OF COST ESCALATION – ROYAL NAVY 1946 TO 1984

Item	Annual change
Increase in budget	2%
Reduced number of ships	$2\frac{1}{2}$%
Saving through increased proportion of smaller types	$4\frac{1}{4}$%
	$8\frac{3}{4}$% (9%)

$(1.02 \times 1.025 \times 1.0425 = 1.0875 \ (1.09)$

The total capability of a fleet is reduced by such changes. There is no escaping the association of cost with performance and armament. Any saving has to be paid for by a loss in capability. The trick is to minimise this loss. A general obsolescence of the whole fleet would mean that it could discharge none of its former missions effectively so that it would cease to be credible in any of the roles to which it might be assigned. On the other hand, a fully up to date complement of some types of ship should enable at least some of the former missions to be discharged as effectively as ever – even if the roles and missions associated with the, now abandoned, more expensive types of ship could no longer be attempted. Since it retains effectiveness in some missions, this is clearly a better option than losing all capability via general obsolescence. It is particularly attractive if the roles that can still be undertaken by the cheaper types of ship are those most essential to vital national interests. Anti-submarine warfare (ASW) in the North Atlantic is an example of a vital role not requiring the most expensive types of warship and is the one upon which the attention of the Royal Navy became increasingly concentrated.

A GENERAL THEORY
There is nothing peculiar to the Royal Navy in a process of changed formation accompanying reduced numerical strength. Rather, the alternative of becoming a miniature version of its former self would have been the unusual course – aside from the obvious difficulty of, say, half a battleship. Throughout history the wealthiest

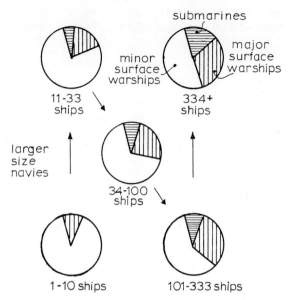

Fig.5 : Bigger navies : bigger ships

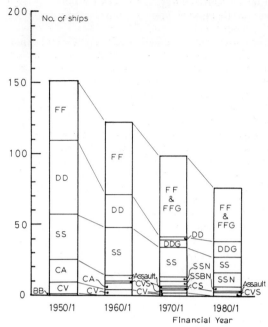

R.N. Active fleet : frigates, submarines & larger vessels

Fig. 6 : Formation of the Royal Navy

nations have aspired to global power while the poorer have had to content themselves with exacting a, hopefully deterrent, price for invasion of their homeland. Such differences in aim were reflected in the formation as well as the composition of their fleets. That this is still so is shown in Fig 5 which summarises data for the world's navies in 1981. It may be seen that the larger and more costly types of warship are the perogative of larger navies while smaller and cheaper types makes up a larger fraction of the numerical strength of small navies.

The coupling of size and formation may profitably be explored a little further in a generalised fashion. To do so we argue along the following lines. The costs of vessels in any navy will be distributed between two limits. At the higher limit are vessels so expensive that any additional cost would cause one of them to absorb too great a proportion of the budget. This maximum will then vary in sympathy with the budget. At the lower limit lie ships that are so small and rudimentary that the reduction in effectiveness necessary for any further reduction in unit cost would deprive them of all military value. This minimum cost will follow the general trend of costs as these are driven upwards with time by military competition. The average unit cost will be intermediate between the upper and lower limits and, hence, will rise at a rate intermediate between the rates of increase of the budget and of the unit costs of any given type of vessel. Its exact value will depend upon the distribution of numbers of ships with their unit cost. An inverse proportionality of numbers with unit cost both makes

the mathematics tractible and, as shown by Augustine, closely approximates many real-life situations. In that case, a 9 per cent per annum growth in unit costs of ships of given type combines with a 2 per cent per annum increase in budget to yield a 4.2 per cent increase in unit cost averaged across the (changing) fleet whose numerical strength declines at 2.6 per cent per annum.

While noting that these mathematical results are remarkably similar to the long-term trends that actually took place (3.2 vs 4¼ and 2.6 vs 2½ per cent), the reader may well wonder as to the value of abstract mathematical results – however neat – to the study of actual events of naval history. The author would reply by recapitulating the assumptions that went into the theory and drawing attention to how few and obvious they were. It was assumed only that ships could be too individually expensive (in relation to the budget) on the one hand and, on the other, could become too rudimentary (in relation to operational needs). It was further assumed that there was a strong tendency to make similar levels of investment in ships of different types (otherwise known as 'preserving a balance fleet') and it was implicitly assumed that ships within the navy were kept fully up to date. There was nothing peculiar to particular designs or to a particular strategy.

If so good a description of actual events flow from so limited and general a set of assumptions then there is the clear implication that a policy maker seeking to preserve an up to date and balanced fleet and to do so within a given budget has only a very restricted range of detailed

TABLE 2: SIZE OF THE ROYAL NAVY ACTIVE FLEET 1948-84
(vessel in commission during year including those used for trials and training)

Financial Year						Type					
Year	(1) SSBN	(2) SSN	(3) SS	(4) BB	(5) CV	(6) CVS	(7) CA &CS	(8) DDG	(9) DD	(10) FF & FFG	(11) LPD & LST
1948/9	–	–	34	4	10	–	18	–	52	43	?
1949/0	–	–	34	5	9	–	17	–	53	44	?
1950/1	–	–	32	1	8	–	16	–	52	42	?
1951/2	–	–	32	1	9	–	15	–	46	49	?
1952/3	–	–	39	1	10	–	14	–	44	55	?
1953/4	–	–	37	1	10	–	13	–	40	48	?
1954/5	–	–	37	1	7	–	11	–	29	54	?
1955/6	–	–	43	1	8 .	–	10	–	31	52	4
1956/7	–	–	42	–	7	–	10	–	32	52	4
1957/8	–	–	39	–	6	–	9	–	30	49	5
1958/9	–	–	38	–	4	–	7	–	26	51	5
1959/0	–	–	36	–	3	–	6	–	25	46	5
1960/	–	–	34	–	4	1	5	–	23	51	4
1961/2	–	–	32	–	4	5	–	22	50	4	
1962/3	–	–	32	–	3	2	4	2	21	50	4
1963/4	–	1	35	–	4	2	3	4	13	52	4
1964/5	–	1	38	–	4	2	4	4	10	53	4
1965/6					(No strength available)						
1966/7	–	3	33	–	4	2	1	6	9	56	2
1967/8	1	3	33	–	3	2	–	6	14	51	2
1968/9	3	2	28	–	2	2	–	6	11	55	2
1969/0	4	3	22	–	2	2	1	6	2	55	2
1970/1	3	3	21	–	2	2	1	5	2	57	2
1971/2	3	4	18	–	2	2	1	7	2	51	2
1972/3	2	6	15	–	1	2	2	6	3	53	2
1973/4	3	8	16	–	1	2	2	8	–	52	2
1974/5					(No Defence White Paper published)						
1975/6	3	5	16	–	1	2	2	10	–	50	2
1976/7	3	7	13	–	1	1	1	9	–	48	1
1977/8	3	6	15	–	1	1	2	9	–	43	1
1978/9	3	9	12	–	1	2	2	13	–	45	1
1979/0	3	9	11	–	–	2	1	12	–	43	1
1980/1	3	110	11	–	–	2	–	11	–	38	1
1981/2	3	8	11	–	–	2	–	14	–	37	1
1982/3	3	9	11	–	–	3	–	14	–	39	1
1983/4	3	9	10	–	–	3	–	13	–	43	1
1984/5	3	10	10	–	–	3	–	16	–	40	1
Falklands task force 1982	–	5	1	–	–	2	–	8	–	15	2

Source of data: Defence White Papers.

Notes

1 Ballistic missile submarines (nuclear powered).

2 Fleet submarines (nuclear powered).

3 Submarines (conventional power) – excluding coastal and miniature types.

4 Battleships

5 Aircraft carriers (multi-purpose) including all carriers operating fixed-wing aircraft with conventional take-off and landing.

6 ASW Aircraft carriers but including all other aircraft carriers operating only helicopters and/or VSTOL aircraft (such as 'commando carriers' etc).

7 Cruisers with guns as primary armament (CA) and helicopter-capable cruisers for ASW (CS).

8 Guided missile destroyers ie destroyers with guided missiles as main armament (in intended roles).

9 Destroyers of all types except DDG.

10 Frigates of all types ie both gun and missile armed and including 'fast frigate' destroyer conversions etc.

11 Assault ships – restricted to major amphibious warfare ships of the LST and, later, LSD types purpose built for use in an initial assault. Excludes both smaller types (LCAC, LCM, LCP etc.) and logistic support ships of all types.

Classification is by contemporary equipment, usage and tasking and not by purposes for which ships may have been designed originally or to which they may have been converted later. For example, *Hermes* initially classified as CV but, after conversion to a 'commando carrier', is later classified as CVS.

Cruisers are all CA type prior to 1967/8 and call CS after that date.

options from which to choose within the framework imposed by adding up the bills. Conversely, the historian must be very cautious in raising questions of 'what might have been' or 'how it might have been done better'. If these depart radically from what has been described for the post-war Royal Navy, there is a strong probability that his suggestions neglect some consequence for cost and/or the balance of the fleet and, hence, its operational effectiveness.

This is not so remarkable a suggestion as it might seem at first sight. In everyday life we are well accustomed to the idea that – unless we accept the risks of great unconventionality – we have only modest freedom for action about the life-style to which our income binds us. Balancing the books while providing for all reasonable needs and contingencies is not different in principle when done in many millions of pounds than it is for everyday life. Income and costs shape the life-style of mighty fleets as they do for individuals.

THE TRANSFORMATION OF THE ROYAL NAVY

We now turn from these broad general principles to consider the details of the transformation undergone by the Royal Navy in the last 40 years.

Even such an apparently straightforward matter as the numbers of each type of vessel in the fleet at various dates is not without its ambiguities when considered over the four decades since World War II. Vessels may be held at any one of a number of states of preparedness for active service while the terminology of their classification into different types has evolved with changes in warship design. In order to present a coherent picture in Table 2, the listings of Royal Navy ships given in successive Defence White Papers have been reinterpreted into the current United States Navy classifications. Further, since we are concerned with the active fleets that were sustained on the monies actually available, only vessels in commission at some time during each financial year (April to March) are included in Table 2 so that this includes vessels engaged on trials and training work at sea but excludes the reserve fleet and ships being constructed or undergoing major refits.

The data given in Table 2 are also presented graphically in Fig 6. They show the working out in practise of the broad trends discussed earlier.

Firstly, the decline in total number of major naval vessels (frigates, fleet submarines and larger) is clearly evident. Secondly, the keeping up to date of the fleet is manifest in the increasing proportion of submarines with nuclear propulsion (SSBN & SSN). This type was first introduced in the Financial year (FY) 1963/4 and it now comprises over half the submarine fleet. Similarly, guided-missile destroyers (DDG) completely supplanted the earlier (DD) designs over the period between FY62/3 and FY73/4 – again indicating a process of keeping up to date.

The change in formation towards a greater proportion of smaller vessels is demonstrated by the larger percentage reductions in numbers of the larger types of ship. This is made explicit in Fig 7 which demonstrates that these reductions have varied progressively from elimina-

tion of the largest types to only modest percentage reductions in the number of frigates.

Finally, it may be noted that the *Invincible* (CVS) cost, in real terms, around 22 per cent more than the *Ark Royal* (CV) so that the unit cost of the largest vessels in the fleet rose at a very modest rate (circa 1 per cent pa) much closer to the 2 per cent pa growth in budget than to the 9 per cent pa growth in unit costs of a given type of ship.

All these observations are in good accord with the earlier deductions from budget totals and cost trends and represent these seen from a more traditional historical standpoint.

ROLES AND MISSIONS

The passing from the Royal Navy of the battleship (BB), cruiser (CA & CS) and the larger conventional aircraft carrier (CV) types were milestones along its evolutionary path and excited public debate.

Reaction to the demise of the big-gun types (BB & CA) was muted by a sense that their day had gone with the maturing, during World War II, of the fleet aircraft carrier as the new capital ship. In this spirit, the counter to the threat posed to ASW convoy escorts by new Russian *Sverdlov* class, gun-armed cruisers was the procurement of 'Buccaneer' strike aircraft. The loss of these types of big-gun ships took some fighting capacity with them if only because, even if an aircraft carrier could do any task formerly assigned to a big-gun ship, no vessel can be in two places at once. However, all the previous capabilities were preserved, if less extensively, which was seen as essential to the discharge of British post-imperial commitments 'east of Suez'.

Subsuming the battleship and cruiser roles into those of the aircraft carrier reinforced the popular contemporary view of the latter as the unrivalled queen of the ocean. This added to the warmth of the debate in the mid-1960s over the abortive proposal for a new generation of such vessels.

At the time it was acknowledged that the phasing out of the fleet carriers and their partial replacements by interim helicopter-capable (CS) ships represented a concentration upon ASW roles and the giving up of the ability to execute an opposed landing outside the range of land-based aircraft. In the event, the introduction of the Sea Harrier VSTOL aircraft conferred the capability of operating fighter aircraft from these smaller vessels and, thus, enabled just such an opposed landing to be effected on the Falklands during 1982. However, while technical innovation softened the impact of this decision, it still remains an excellent example of the way in which rising costs increasingly constrain the types of vessel that even a major navy can maintain in service and, hence, enforce changes in its capabilities, roles and missions. In turn, such changes impact upon national policy. The cancellation of the replacement fleet carriers was linked with a withdrawal from roles 'east of Suez' – evidenced by the rapid changes in deployment of the British Army shown in Fig 8.

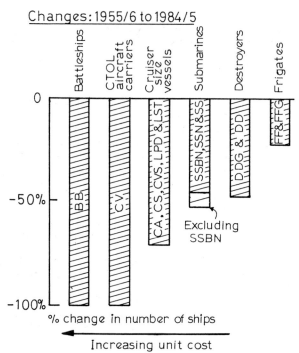

Changes: 1955/6 to 1984/5

Battleships — BB

CTOL aircraft carriers — CV

Cruiser size vessels — CA, CS, CVS, LPD & LST

Submarines — SSBN, SSN & SS

Destroyers — DDG & DD

Frigates — FF & FFG

Excluding SSBN

0

−50%

−100%

% change in number of ships

← Increasing unit cost

Fig: 7 Where the cuts fell

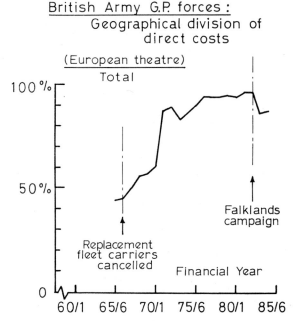

British Army G.P. forces:
Geographical division of direct costs

(European theatre)
Total

100 %

50 %

0

60/1   65/6   70/1   75/6   80/1   85/6

Financial Year

Replacement fleet carriers cancelled

Falklands campaign

Fig. 8: Epilogue of Empire

CONCLUSION

Rising unit costs are inevitable if a fleet is to be kept up to date and effective relative to potential opponents. Such escalation in unit costs has moulded the post-war evolution of all fleets including the Royal Navy. While increases in budget and reductions in the number of ships have occurred, an equally important contribution to containing expenditures within budgets has been made by the changing formation of the fleet. This has evolved towards a greater proportion of the smaller types of vessel and the complete phasing out of the largest types. While this has necessitated concentration upon a reduced set of missions, it is clearly preferable to the alternative of fleet-wide obsolesence with consequent failure to discharge any mission effectively.

Within this context the most significant post-war technical innovation has been the advent of the Harrier VSTOL aircraft. This has greatly ameliorated the reduction in capabilities that were thought at the time to flow from the decision to abandon the operation of large conventional aircraft carriers by the Royal Navy. By reintroducing the ability to operate fighter aircraft it preserved the capability for amphibious warfare – as so convincingly demonstrated during 1982 in the South Atlantic.

Certainly, popular commentators are wrong when they conclude from simplistic comparisons of, say, the numbers and size of ships at successive Spithead reviews that the Royal Navy has declined almost to impotence since World War II. They are doubly wrong when they ascribe this alleged change to sharply reduced spending

on the Navy. Rather, the post-war transformation of the Royal Navy has been a logical and highly successful response to the problems of keeping it fully effective in its most vital roles despite the clash between the rapid rise in unit costs and a more slowly growing budget.

SOURCES

The numerical data on strengths, formations and budgets of the Royal Navy have been taken from post-war Defence White Papers or from the summaries of earlier ones given in *The decline of British seapower* by D Western (Janes, London 1982) – an excellent comprehensive account even if this author cannot concur in the judgement implicit in its title.

Trends in unit costs are described in the present author's earlier article 'Of Ships and money': the rising cost of naval power', *Warship* 32, October 1984. Information on other navies came from *The War Atlas* by M Kidron & D Smith (Pan, London, 1983). Contemporary views of policy came from Defence White Papers and the works of N Friedman – especially his history of equipment and policy in *Carrier Air Power* (Conway, London, 1981).

Further background to the problems of defence procurement is to be found in 'Towards the Starship Enterprise – are the current trends in defence unit costs inexorable?' by D L I Kirkpatrick & P G Pugh (*Aerospace*, Royal Aeronautical Society, London, May 1983) and the witty and most perceptive book by N R Augustine entitled *Augustine's Laws* (American Institute of Aeronautics and Astronautics, New York, 1984). For the long-term historical perspective see 'Determinants of the British Defence Burden, 1689-1977' by G Kohler (*Bulletin of Peace Proposals* (1), 1980).

Motor Minesweeper 191

by The Rev Michael Melvin

With the passing of 40 years, warships from World War II have become a rare species. Some larger vessels have been preserved, but many of the smaller craft passed into mercantile service and were worn out in peaceful activity.

Caledonian MacBrayne's M V *Loch Arkaig* was built in 1941 and as MMS 46 spent most of her time in the Mediterranean. The Dutch Brigantine *Elizabeth Smit* as MMS 54 was one of eight ships of the same class which finished their time with the Royal Netherlands Navy.

These were but two of the 313 short hull wooden minesweepers planned to counter the growing menace of the magnetic and acoustic mines of World War II. In fact there were only about 250 involved, for many were never completed because of enemy action (mostly those building overseas in Burma and Hong Kong as well as Singapore) and a number of those ordered in the latter years of the war were cancelled.

Of those which did see service, the majority were built in yards all around the British coastline, anywhere in fact which could deal with this kind of task. About 40 vessels were built in Canada.

There are 47 Flotillas of the 105-foot class, operating in most of the major ports around the coast, but mainly in the North Sea and English Channel, and the ships were manned by personnel of the Royal Naval Patrol Service, based at Lowestoft. Commanding Officers were either Royal Naval Reserve or from the Royal Naval Volunteer Reserve, many of whom had never seen a vessel of this kind in their lives, let alone command one.

Most of the time was spent in routine sweeps, that is, keeping the shipping lanes open. It was for the most part a soul destroying and monotonous task: out sweeps and in sweeps from one day to the next, and very often at night. The ships were not very well armed; in the early days, twin 0.5s aft of the bridge and twin Lewis guns on the port and starboard bridge wings. It was not until later in the war that 20mm Oerlikons were fitted fore and aft. The vessels were sitting ducks for enemy aircraft or indeed for shore batteries during the sweeping of the French and Dutch shorelines, long before 'D' Day ever commenced. With a maximum speed of 11 knots flat out, there was little chance of getting out of the way. They had the advantage of being small so perhaps a little more difficult to hit than the larger vessels, but nevertheless there were many near misses, judging from the records. During the 'D' Day operations most of the flotillas had some involvement as the task grew bigger. The channels had to be kept clear, and this meant working round the clock. One minesweeper, unable to return to the UK following the cancellation on the night of 5 June, hid up behind the St Marcouf Islands just off the coast of Brittany. The crew could actually hear the Germans speaking ashore.

Much of the sweeping was a hit and miss affair, with a great deal of trial and error, following the discovery of a magnetic mine in the mud off Shoeburyness.

Very little if anything has ever been said about the role of the MMS, without which and others like them the war could not have been effectively fought. The ships covered hundreds of thousands of miles right around the world, to keep the shipping lanes clear. One flotilla covered 10,000 miles alone sweeping up and down the River Forth. The crews and ships, apart from the odd congratulatory signal were given little or no credit at all. The commemoration of Operation 'Overlord' last year mentioned nothing of the task the sweepers had to accomplish, and forgot to mention one of the most difficult operations in the war – 'Kalendar', the clearing of the River Schelde.

In all, 60 of this particular type of craft were either lost or damaged during hostilities, their crews remembered each year at a Memorial Service held in Lowestoft in October, when over 500 Royal Naval Patrol Service members pay their respects.

Following the war many of the ships found their way into private hands and many dispersed to different parts of the world, like MMS 102 which ended up in the Falklands, or MMS 46 which is now sailing under the Dubai flag. These ships and crews did an excellent job in the war against unknown odds, and many continued their minesweeping activities till long after the war was over. Others ended up in the breakers yard, their hulls burned after all the valuable items had been removed. The only ship of this class still in her original condition is MMS 191, discovered by the writer while researching for a book.

She was found in one of the creeks up the River Medway, was purchased by the founder of the Motor Minesweeper Trust in 1979, and is now being restored as far as cash will allow in the only place available which does not charge the earth for berthing facilities. The fact that she lies in tidal waters in the saltings of Stoke Creek provides its own problems, but over the last four years work has been done to preserve what must be quite an historic vessel.

The trials and tribulations attached to the ship's discovery and subsequent removal of her new berth are now legend, but the work continues progressively by a few dedicated members of the Trust plus the occasional help of the Sea Cadets based in Harlow town. We have learned through trial and error how to cope with the work which needs to be done. It took four years to find a set of drawings (with no help at all from MoD (Navy) in spite of repeated requests), but help was offered from sources who were once our enemies.

When Chatham Dockyard was destined to close, one might have thought that help with chandlery might be forthcoming, but even with the help of the Rear Admiral Medway, we received nothing, and it was at Chatham that all the surplus sweepers were held in reserve and from which they were all disposed.

The MMS Trust believes that MMS 191 should be fully restored for historical reasons primarily because she is the last ship of a particular line, and also to give practical training to Sea Cadets in engineering and seamanship.

The builders of MMS 191, McDuff Shipbuilding and Engineering of McDuff Scotland, advise that a new ship of this kind would cost at today's rates, £1 million, and to restore the present vessel to a sea-going capacity £250,000.

1 Ex MMS 54, now the Dutch brigantine *Elizabeth Smith*.
Author's Collection

2 Ex MMS 46, now the M/V *Loch Arkaig*.
Author's Collection

3 MMS 191 as the Belgian M944 during the post war clearance of the River Scheldt.
Author's Collection

4 MMS during the war, and undergoing restoration on the Medway.
Author's Collection

5 Ex MMS 102 lying in the Falkland Islands in 1984.
Author's Collection

Ships of the line of the Spanish Navy (1714-1825)

by C de Saint Hubert

INTRODUCTION

By the end of the War of the Spanish Succession, the great naval power which Spain had enjoyed in the sixteenth and seventeenth centuries had ended.

The Royal Navy of Spain was founded in 1714. Before that date there had been not one unified Spanish Navy, but up to 12 regional or provincial naval forces.

During the eighteenth century a number of remarkable Ministers of Marine rebuilt Spain's naval power: Patiño (1717–1736), Marquis de la Ensenada (1737–1754), Arriaga (1754–1775), Castejon (1776–1783), Valdés (1783–1795). They not only build ships but also provided the navy with a good organisation and the required infrastructure. Fortified naval bases and arsenals (dock-yards) were thus built at Ferrol, Carraca (near Cadiz) and Cartagena. Two other important dock-yards were set up at Havana and Guarnizo (near Santander). Ships-of-the-line built at: Havana: 60; Ferrol 41; Guarnizo 34; Cartagena 20; Carraca (Cadiz) 6.

During most of the eighteenth century the Spanish Navy was the world's third largest, after the Royal Navy and the French Navy (which, at times, it almost equalled).

In 1793 Spain had 76 ships-of-the-line, 50 frigates, 9 corvettes and a number of lesser units (including 'jabeques', specially built craft, fast and well-armed, to fight the North African pirates in the Mediterranean). The French Navy then had 81 ships-of-the-line and about 70 frigates. As to the Royal Navy its strength was superior to the combined strength of France and Spain: 141 ships-of-the-line, 19 fifty-gun ships, 117 frigates, etc.

From 1793 to 1825 Spain was almost continually at war. At the end of this period the country and the navy were ruined. In 1825 the Spanish Navy only had 6 ships-of-the-line, 7 frigates and 9 corvettes.

The main factors which brought about the downfall of Spain as a major naval power after 1793 were:

a Almost permanent warfare; viz against France (1793-1795), against Britain (1796-1802), against Britain again (1804-1808), and against France (1808-1814).

b From 1808 to 1814 the greater part of Spain was occupied by French troops and a fierce contest raged, on Spanish territory, between the French army and Spanish forces. The latter were made up of both regular forces (including a number of naval battalions) and irregular troops (guerrillas).

c As a consequence of the French invasion of Spain, insurrections broke out in various parts of the Spanish Empire in America. From 1809 to 1825 Spain gradually lost all her American possessions, with the exception of Cuba and Porto Rico. This loss was of great financial importance since, for a long time, the minerals produced by her American colonies had been one of the mainstays of the Spanish exchequer.

d The state of the Spanish arsenals after 1793 deserves a special mention. Continuous warfare soon depleted the dockyards' stores and capabilities and these could not be made good due to the fact that the wars taxed Spain's financial resources to the utmost and disrupted her administrative machinery. Of course, the French invasion of 1808 made matters even worse. From 1793 to 1825 the Spanish Navy lost 22 ships-of-the-line in action or as a direct consequence thereof, 10 ships were wrecked, 8 ships were transferred to France and 39 ships were stricken. Many of the latter were not over age and should normally have had a longer career had the dockyards been able to maintain and repair them properly. A total 79 units were thus lost, transferred or stricken during the period.

To offset these losses only 11 ships-of-the-line were commissioned in the Spanish Navy between 1793 and 1815. Of these six were French ships captured in Spanish harbours at the time of the French invasion (1808) and only two ships and two frigates (not counting those already on the stocks in 1793) were built by the dockyards. This figure compares most unfavourably with that of Spain's four main arsenals (Ferrol, Havana, Cartagena, Cadiz) during the previous period. From 1780 to 1793, 31 ships-of-the-line and 43 frigates were built. After 1815, five Russian ships-of-the-line were acquired but they were found to be rotten!

NOTES ABOUT THE OPERATIONAL DATA

From 1714 to 1825[1] the Spanish Navy had 226 ships-of-the-line (s/l). Sixty-two of these were lost in action or as a direct consequence thereof (eg scuttled or burned to prevent capture by the enemy, wrecked after heavy battle damage, etc).

The main battles and actions of the Spanish Navy during the period were (the number in brackets after the date indicates the number of s/l's lost):

A. Battle of Cape Pessaro (1718) (7)
B. Defence of Cartagena de Indias (1741) (6)
C. Battle of Cape Sicie (or of Toulon) (1744) (1)
D. Action off Havana (1748) (2)

E. Defense of Havana (1762) (12)
F. Battle of Cape Sta Maria (1780) (6)
G. Battle of Cape St Vincent (1797) (4)
H. Defense of Trinidad (1797) (4)
I. Action Off Gibraltar (1801) (2)
J. Action off Cape Finisterre (1805) (2)
K. Battle of Trafalgar (1805) (10)

[1]In 1714 the Spanish Navy was reorganised as a single force as opposed to the 10 to 12 more or less independent squadrons which made up the Spanish Navy in the sixteenth and seventeenth centuries.
    In 1825 the colonial war in Latin America came to an end and Spain was at peace for the first time since 1793 (except for short periods in 1795-96 and 1802-03). These 32 years of continuous warfare brought about the ruin of Spain and of her navy. In 1793 Spain has 76 s/l and 50 frigates; in 1825 only 6 s/l and 7 frigates were left.

A. Battle of Cape Passaro (11 August 1718) A British fleet of 22 s/l (Admiral Byng) unexpectedly attacked a Spanish Fleet (12 s/l and a few frigates) (Admiral Gastañeta). Britain and Spain were not at war.

List of the Spanish s/l
1 *San Felipe el Real* (1) (flagship) (70/80) Captured
2 *Principe de Asturias* (1) (70) Captured
3 *Sta Isabel* (1) (60) Captured
4 *San Carlos* (1) (60) Captured
5 *San Isidro* (1) (50) Captured
6 *Sta Rosa* (56) Captured
7 *Real Mazi* (56) Captured
8 *San Fernando* (1) (60)
9 *San Luis* (1) (60)
10 *San Pedro* (1) (60)
11 *San Juan Bautista* (1) (60)
12 *Hermione* (50)

B. Defense of Cartagena de Indias (March-May 1741) The British under Admiral Vernon attacked and besieged Cartagena with 36 s/l, 12 frigates and 12,000 troops. The Spanish had 6 s/l in the harbour and some 2000 troops. The British were unable to capture this important Spanish base and trading city and, after incurring heavy losses, had to raise the siege. The Spanish Admiral Blas de Lezo, who gallantly defended the city, died of wounds.

Lists of the Spanish s/l
1 *San Carlos* (2) (66) Used as floating battery then scuttled to block the entrance of the harbour
2 *Conquistador* (2) (62) Id
3 *Africa*)1) (64) Id
4 *Dragon* (1) (64) Id
5 *Galicia* (1) (70) Id, raised by the British renamed 'Galicia Prize', scuttled by the British when they left
6 *San Felipe* (2) (70) Burned to prevent capture by the British

C. Battle of Cape Sicie (or of Toulon) (21-23 February 1744) Between a combined fleet of 17 French s/l and 12

Real Felipe, 114 guns, built at Guarnizo in 1732.
Author's Collection

Spanish s/l and a British Fleet of 32 s/l which was blockading Toulon. The Admirals were: Navarro (Spain), Court de la Bruyère (France) and Mathews (Britain).

List of the Spanish s/l
1 *Real Felipe* (flagship) (114)
2 *Sta Isabel* (2) (80)
3 *Constante* (2) (66)
4 *San Fernando* (2) (64)
5 *Oriente* (1) (60)
6 *America* (1) (60)
7 *Neptuno* (60)
8 *Hercules* (64)
9 *Brillante* (60)
11 *Halcon* (60)
11 *Soberbio* (1) (60)
12 *Poder* (60) Captured by the British, recaptured by the Spanish and burned to prevent recapture by the British

D. Action off Havana (12 October 1748) Between 6 Spanish s/l (Admiral Reggio) and 7 British s/l (Admiral Knowles). The Spanish squadron was defending a convoy.

List of the Spanish s/l
1 *Africa* (2) (70) (flagship) Run aground and burned to prevent capture

A Spanish 74-gun ship of the line.
Author's Collection

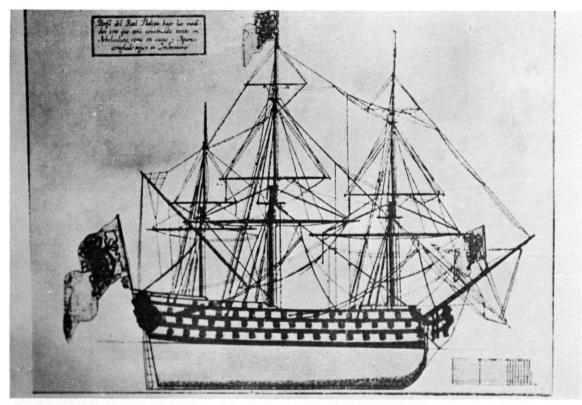

Real Felipe during the battle of Toulon, 1744.
Author's Collection

2 *Invencible* (2) (70)
3 *Conquistador* (3) (60) Captured
4 *Dragon* (2) (60)
5 *Nueva España* (1) (60)
6 *Real Familia* (60)

E. Defense of Havana (7 June-10 August 1762) A British force (26 s/l, 15 frigates and 12,000 troops) under Admiral Pocock attacked, besieged and finally captured Havana which was gallantly defended by the Spanish. The soul of the defense was Captain Velasco who died of wounds at the end of the siege. The Spanish had 12 s/l in the harbour and 2800 troops to defend Havana.

List of the Spanish s/l
 1 *Neptuno* (2) (70) Scuttled to block the harbour entrance
 2 *Europa* (1) (60) Id.
 3 *Asia* (2) (60) Id.
 4 *America* (1) (60) Captured
 5 *Tigre* (70) Captured
 6 *Reina* (2) (70) Captured
 7 *Infante* (2) (70) Captured
 8 *Soberano* (2) (70) Captured
 9 *Aquilon* (70) Captured
10 *Conquistador* (4) (60) Captured
11 *San Antonio* (2) (60) Captured
12 *San Genero* (1) (60) Captured

Two s/l building at Havana, *San Carlos* (80) and *Santiago* (60), were destroyed on the stocks by the British before leaving. The Arsenal was laid waste but it was soon repaired (from 1765 on s/l and frigates were again being launched at Havana).

F. Battle of Cape Sta Maria ('Moonlight' or 1st Cape St Vincent) (16 January 1780) During the Great Siege of Gibraltar, between a British fleet of 21 s/l and 9 frigates (Admiral Rodney) and a Spanish fleet of 11 s/l and 2 frigates (Admiral de Langara).

List of the Spanish s/l
 1 *Fenix* (flagship) (80) Captured
 2 *Princesa* (2) (74) Captured
 3 *Diligente* (74) Captured
 4 *Monarca* (1) (74) Captured
 5 *Sto Domingo* (1) (74) blew up (1 survivor!)
 6 *San Julian* (1) (64) Captured by the British, recaptured by her crew, wrecked 2 days later due to heavy battle damage.
 7 *San Agustin* (74)
 8 *San Lorenzo* (74)
 9 *San Eugenio* (74)
10 *San Genaro* (2) (74)
11 *San Justo* (2) (74)

G. Battle of Cape St Vincent (14 February 1797) Between a Spanish fleet of 25 s/l (Admiral de Cordoba) and a British fleet of 15 s/l (Admiral Jervis).

List of the Spanish s/l
 1 *Santisima Trinidad* (flag) (130)

2 *Concepcion* (112)
3 *Principe de Asturias* (112)
4 *Conde de Regla* (112)
5 *Mejicano* (112)
6 *San Jose* (112) Captured
7 *Salvador del Mundo* (112) Captured
8 *San Nicolas* (80) Captured
9 *Neptuno* (3) (80)
10 *Bahama* (74)
11 *San Isidor* (74) Captured
12 *Oriente* (74)
13 *Atlante* (74)
14 *San Genaro* (74)
15 *San Juan Nepomuceno* (74)
16 *San Pablo* (74)
17 *San Fermin* (74)
18 *San Ildefonso* (74)
19 *San Antonio* (74)
20 *San Francisco de Paula* (74)
21 *Soberano* (2) (74)
22 *Conquistador* (5) (74)
23 *Pelayo* (74)
24 *Terrible* (74)
25 *Santo Domingo* (68)

H. Defense of Trinidad (February 1797) Attack and capture of Trinidad by a British force (9 s/l, 3 frigates, and 6800 troops) under Admiral Harvey and General Abercromby. The Spanish had 4 s/l & 1 frigate under Admiral Ruiz de Apodaca.

List of the Spanish s/l
1 *San Vicente* (80 Burned to prevent capture
2 *Arrogante* (74) Id.
3 *Gallardo* (74) Id.
4 *San Damaso* (74) (Scuttled to block harbour entrance, raised by the British)

I. Action off Gibraltar (12 July 1801) Between a combined squadron of 5 Spanish s/l (+ 1 frigate) (Admiral Moreno) and 4 French s/l (+ 2 frigates) (Admiral Linois) and a British squadron of 5 s/l (+ 1 frigate) (Admiral Saumarez).

List of the Spanish s/l
1 *Real Carlos* (112) Blew up (about 20 survivors)
2 *San Hermenegildo* (112) Blew up (about 20 survivors)
3 *San Fernando* (94)
4 *Argonauta* (74)
5 *San Agustin* (74)

J. Action off Cape Finisterre (22 July 1805) Also called 'Calder's Action (by the British) and 'Combat des Quinze-Vingts' (by French))
Between a combined fleet of 14 French s/l (Admiral Villeneuve) and 6 Spanish s/l (Admiral Gravina) and a British fleet of 15 s/l (Admiral Calder).

List of the Spanish s/l
1 *Firme* (74) Captured
2 *San Rafael* (74) Captured
3 *America* (2) (74)
4 *España* (1) (64)
5 *Terrible* (74)
6 *Argonauta* (1) (80)

K. Battle of Trafalgar (21 October 1805) Between a combined fleet composed of 18 French s/l (Admiral Villeneuve) and 15 Spanish s/l (Admiral Gravina, who later died of wounds) and Nelson's fleet of 27 s/l.

List of the Spanish s/l
1 *Principe de Asturias* (112) (flagship
2 *Santa Ana* (112) Captured by the British, recaptured by her crew
3 *Santisima Trinidad* (136) – Captured by the British, sank in the storm which followed the battle.
4 *Rayo* (80) Heavily damaged, wrecked in the storm
5 *Argonauta* (80) Captured, sank in the storm
6 *Montañes* (74)
7 *Neptuno* (3) (80) Captured, recaptured by her crew, wrecked in the storm
8 *San Agustin* (80) Captured then burned by the British
9 *San Juan Nepomuceno* (74) Captured
10 *San Ildefonso* (74) Captured
11 *Bahama* (74)
12 *Monarca* (2) (74) Captured, later sank in the storm
13 *San Justo* (2) (74)
14 *San Leandro* (2) (64)
15 *San Francisco de Asis* (74) Heavily damaged, sank in the storm   *To be continued.*

book reviews

US CRUISERS
An Illustrated Design History
by Norman Friedman
Published by Arms & Armour Press
8½in × 11in 576pp, 250 illustrations.
ISBN 0 85368 651 3 (£27.50)

Norman Friedman needs no introduction to readers of *Warship*. In this volume he continues the work begun in the Destroyer and Aircraft carrier volumes, and, as before, it is work of the highest quality. He combines naval design and technology with a clear grasp of overall naval policy and the political influences that effect it. This book cannot be recommended too highly.

AMERICAN NAVAL HISTORY
by Jack Seetman
Published by The United States Naval Institute Press
8½in × 11in 330pp, over 200 illustrations.
ISBN 0 87021 290 7

An illustrated chronology from 1775 to 1984. This well constructed reference book is of greatest interest, especially for the less well known areas of American history, the struggles with the Algerian corsairs, interventions in Mexico and the naval aspects of the Civil War. All are made comprehensible and interesting, with a wealth of good illustrations.

SHIPS AND AIRCRAFT OF THE US FLEET: 13th EDITION
by Norman Polmar
Published by Arms & Armour Press
10in × 10in, 448pp, 800+ photographs and Drawings
ISBN 0 85368 701 3 (£23.50)

The new edition of this well known and highly regarded work brings it up to date with details of the 'Aegis' cruisers of the 'Ticonderoga' class and the refitted battleships of the 'Iowa' class. Work on vertical launch missile systems and new attack submarines is also included.

NORTH ATLANTIC RUN
The Royal Canadian Navy and the battle for the convoys
by Marc Milner
Published by The University of Toronto Press, July 1985
235mm × 160mm, 326pp, 30 illustrations, bibliography, index.
ISBN 0 8020 2544 7 (£18.95)

Author Marc Milner must be congratulated on a first-class book. He begins by examining the pre-war origins of Canadian Naval Policy and develops into an account of the convoy battles and their effect on the structure of the RCN. The often criticised performance of the Canadian escort groups is treated in the light of the dramatic expansion of the RCN, its inability to match the RN in fitting modern sensors and weapons and the need to hold the line in 1942 with half trained crews.

This book is based on a wealth of original research, which the author has handled skilfully. It is also well written, clear and informative. It will remain the standard account for years to come.

U-BOATS AGAINST CANADA
German submarines in Canadian waters
by Michael L Hadley
Published by McGill-Queen's, May 1985
235mm × 160mm (9¼in × 6in), 360pp, 39 illustrations, bibliography, index, etc.
ISBN 0 7735 0584 0 ($29.95 Canadian)

Using German and Canadian archives and interviews with survivors Captain Hadley builds up a detailed account of the German submarine operations that penetrated Canadian coastal waters especially those that entered the St Lawrence seaway.

The conclusions to this book echo those of Milner, whose work features in another excellent bibliography. These two books complement one another, without overlapping; both are excellent.

BALTIC ASSIGNMENT
Briitsh Submariners in Russia: 1914-1919
by Michael Wilson
Published by Leo Cooper/Secker & Warburg, April 1985
220mm × 140mm, 244pp, 28 illustrations, index.
ISBN 0 436 57801 8 (£13.95)

Warship contributor Michael Wilson has produced a balanced account of the activity of the eight British submarines that operated in the Baltic during the First World War. Their neglected campaign had a powerful effect on the Germans who, frightened by the threat to their iron ore supplies from Sweden, instituted a convoy system to counter the British successes.

The history of Russia in the War and Revolution is examined, to emphasise the troubled background to the operations of Captain Cromie and his men. They were only a small element in the tragedy, but they do provide a fascinating account of just what was wrong with Czarist Russia.

The account of how the Admiralty decided to send the submarines reveals just how amateur the conduct of the early months of the war really was.

ALLIED LANDING CRAFT OF WORLD WAR TWO
introduced by A D Baker III
Published by Arms & Armour Press 1985
240mm × 170mm, 208pp, 445 illustrations.
ISBN 0 85368 687 4 (£11.95)

This reprint of the US Naval Intelligence manual provides a comprehensive and accurate listing of the specialist Amphibious Warfare craft used by the Allies. Ranging from converted liners to open boats it also includes a wide variety of modifications, notably the LCG(L)3 armed with two 4.7in low-angle guns and the LCF (2) with two twin 4in AA mounts. Furthermore, it is a remarkable record of the specifically wartime development of these vessels and the astounding productive capacity of the USA, where the majority of them were built. Industrial vitality of this order secured victory in both World Wars.

PIGBOAT 39
An American Submarine goes to War
by Bobette Guigliotta
Published by University of Kentucky Press 1984
235mm × 160mm, 224pp, illustrated.
ISBN 0 8131 1524 8 (£19.50)

The obsolete Submarine *S 39* was a part of the US Asiatic Fleet based at Manilla when the war broke out. This book follows her from there to shipwreck off the coast of Australia in August 1942. In between times she sank two Japanese merchant ships and patrolled out of Soerabaya in the Dutch East Indies. On another level it is also an attempt to explain why the Allies were so easily beaten by the Japanese, Dutch indifference and American unpreparedness.

Andrew Lambert

Dear Dr Lambert,
Have you any connection with Mr Lambert, a British engineer, who was appointed in 1859 for one year (till 20 September 1860) the chief-engineer of the Baltic Fleet with a payment £1500 per year. His main duties were to keep the steamers of the Baltic Fleet serviceable and moreover to prepare materials (documents) for modernisation of the Russian naval marine engineering. He was found in England and recommended to the General-Admiral by Admiral Graf Putyanin. According to a separate contract also Mr Lee was employed to translate all papers of Mr Lambert.
Hoping to hear from you soon.
Yours very truly,
Andrej v. Mach
Gdansk-Oliwa
Poland

Hood (*Warship* 34 p80) from Lieutenant J V P Goldrick RAN. The pictorial on *Hood* is a good one, but the caption to the last photograph is misleading. Hailie Sellassie is flanked, *not* by Admirals, but by the Captain of the Ship – on the left of the photo – and a Vice Admiral, whom I presume to be S R Bailey. It is in any case NOT Pound. Further, the negative is the wrong way round – the photo shows the *starboard* side of the ship. The give away comes in the uniforms – the ribbons are the wrong way round. (They are certainly not for lifesaving).

NAVAL BOOKS

Conway Maritime offer an unrivalled range of authoritative and well-illustrated titles on naval subjects. A free catalogue is available, but some of the leading titles are listed below:

CONWAY'S ALL THE WORLD'S FIGHTING SHIPS

This four-volume series covers the history of iron and steel warships from the first ironclad until the present day. Each volume contains a complete listing of all warships from the period, illustrated with numerous photographs and line drawings. The introduction and class notes contain both a major revaluation of published information and the wide-scale use of unpublished sources recently made available for the first time.

CONWAY'S ALL THE WORLD'S FIGHTING SHIPS 1860-1905*
310 x 216mm (12¼" x 8½"), 440 pages, 471 photographs, 506 line drawings. ISBN 0 85177 133 5.
£30.00 (+ £3.00 p & p)

CONWAY'S ALL THE WORLD'S FIGHTING SHIPS 1906-21*
310 x 216mm (12¼" x 8½"), 440 pages, 400 photographs, 600 line drawings. ISBN 0 85177 245 5.
£35.00 (+ £3.50 p & p)

CONWAY'S ALL THE WORLD'S FIGHTING SHIPS 1922 -1946*
310 x 216mm (12¼" x 8½"), 464 pages, 506 photographs, 530 line drawings. ISBN 0 85177 146 7.
£30.00 (+ £3.00 p & p)

CONWAY'S ALL THE WORLD'S FIGHTING SHIPS 1947 -1982*
Part I: The Western Powers
Part II: The Warsaw Pact and non-aligned nations
Each part: 310 x 216mm (12¼" x 8½"), 256 pages, 250 photographs, 240 line drawings.
Part I: ISBN 0 85177 225 0.
£25.00 (+ £2.50 p & p)
Part II: ISBN 0 85177 278 1.
£25.00 (+ £2.50 p & p)

ANATOMY OF THE SHIP SERIES

This new series is a radical departure from the usual monograph approach for each volume contains, as well as text and photographs, a complete set of superbly executed line drawings, both the conventional type of plan as well as explanatory perspective views; this, combined with a full design and service history for the vessel and a photographic section concentrating on close-ups and on-board shots, provides the enthusiast with a novel insight into the technicalities of each ship type covered.
Published so far :

THE BATTLECRUISER HOOD*
John Roberts
240 x 254mm (9½" x 10") landscape, 128 pages, 24 photographs, 320 line drawings. ISBN 0 85177 250 1.
£8.50 (+ £1.25 p & p)

THE AIRCRAFT CARRIER INTREPID*
John Roberts
240 x 254mm (9½" x 10") landscape, 96 pages, 20 photographs, 300 line drawings. ISBN 0 85177 250 1.
£8.50 (+ £1.25 p & p)

THE TYPE VII U-BOAT*
David Westwood
240 x 254mm (9½" x 10") landscape, 96 pages, 20 photographs, 300 line drawings. ISBN 0 85177 314 1.
£9.50 (+ £1.25 p & p)

THE FAIRMILE 'D' TYPE MOTOR TORPEDO BOAT*
John Lambert
240 x 254mm (9½" x 10") landscape, 96 pages, 20 photographs, 300 line drawings. ISBN 0 85177 321 4.
£11.95 (+ £1.50 p & p)

THE DESTROYER ESCORT ENGLAND*
Al Ross
240 x 254mm (9½" x 10") landscape, 96 pages, 20 photographs, 300 line drawings. ISBN 0 85177 325 7.
£10.95 (+ £1.25 p & p)

THE CRUISER BELFAST*
Ross Watton
240 x 254mm (9½" x 10") landscape, 96 pages, 20 photographs, 300 line drawings. ISBN 0 85177 328 1.
£11.95 (+ £1.50 p & p)

* These titles are available in North America from the Naval Institute Press, Annapolis, MD 21402.

From your local bookseller or by post from **Conway Maritime Press Ltd,** 24 Bride Lane, Fleet Street, London EC4Y 8DR

NAVAL WEAPONS OF WORLD WAR II
John Campbell
Completely encyclopaedic in scope, this new reference book covers guns, mountings, torpedoes, mines, anti-submarine and aerial weapons and the earliest naval missiles. Written by a regular contributor to *Warship, Naval Weapons of World War II* must be regarded as one of the most important naval reference works in recent years.
310 x 216mm (12¼" x 8½"), 416 pages,250 photographs, 300 line drawings. ISBN 0 85177 329 X.
£30.00 (+ £3.00 p & p)

CONWAY'S DIRECTORY OF MODERN NAVAL POWER 1986
Edited by Hugh Cowin
This new compendium is designed to be more manageable than the huge and very expensive yearbooks, but at the same time to incorporate all the information needed for a proper appraisal of each navy. Equal weight is given to naval aircraft and weapons systems as to the warships themselves, thus obviating the necessity of consulting three or four different manuals.
310 x 216mm (12¼" x 8¼"), 288 pages, 500 photographs, 100 line drawings. ISBN 0 85177 362 1.
£25.00 (+ £2.50 p & p)

SUBMARINES WITH WINGS
The Past, Present and Future of Aircraft-carrying Submarines
Terry Treadwell
The value of launching scout and reconnaissance aircraft from plat-forms which could then submerge has long been recognised, though the most spectacular example was probably the Japanese attack on the Panama canal in 1945. These early efforts have been well documented in this essentially pictorial book, which also carries the story up to the present day.
240 x 184mm (9½" x 7¼"), 144 pages, 110 photographs, 15 line drawings. ISBN 0 85177 369 9.
£11.95 (+ £1.80 p & p)

THE CUXHAVEN RAID
The World's First Naval Air Strike
R D Layman
The full fascinating story of the world's first naval air strike, on Christmas Day, 1914 when a small and very mixed force of British sea-planes was launched from their carriers to attack the German airship base near Cuxhaven. A highly significant event, told in detail for the first time.
221 x 156mm (9½" x 6"), 160 pages, 40 illustrations. ISBN 0 85177 327 3.
£10.50 (+ £1.25 p & p)

When ordering direct please add the posting and packing charge noted after the price.